TURNING BOWLS
WITH RICHARD RAFFAN

TURNING BOWLS

WITH RICHARD RAFFAN

The Taunton Press

The Taunton Press, Inc., 63 South Main Street, PO Box 5506, Newtown, CT 06470-5506
e-mail: tp@taunton.com

Distributed by Publishers Group West

DESIGN: Rosalind Wanke
LAYOUT: Suzie Yannes
ILLUSTRATOR: Michael Gellatly
COVER AND INTERIOR PHOTOGRAPHER: Richard Raffan

LIBRARY OF CONGRESS CATALOGING-IN-PUBLICATION DATA:
Raffan, Richard.
     Turning bowls with Richard Raffan.
        p.   cm.
     Includes index.
     ISBN 1-56158-508-4
     1. Turning.   2. Bowls (Tableware).   I. Title.

TT201 .R3376   2002
684'.08–dc21   2001054013

Printed in the United States of America
10 9 8 7 6 5 4 3 2 1

ABOUT YOUR SAFETY

Working wood is inherently dangerous. Using hand or power tools improperly or ignoring safety practices can lead to permanent injury or even death. Don't try to perform operations you learn about here (or elsewhere) unless you're certain they are safe for you. If something about an operation doesn't feel right, don't do it. Look for another way. We want you to enjoy the craft, so please keep safety foremost in your mind whenever you're in the shop.

To all those who never cease striving to do

whatever they do as well as possible and then better.

Acknowledgments

Thank you to all my students and the collectors I have met:

I hope you've learned as much from me as I have from you. And thanks

to Rick Mastelli for a most enjoyable editing experience.

Contents

Introduction

I began turning wood in January 1970, and after more than 30 years I continue to enjoy making bowls. Mostly I relish the quest for truly satisfying forms but, like most turners, I also find addictive the rush of shavings from the tool and the magical way dull surfaces come to life in a few seconds when oiled and waxed.

It is no wonder, to me, that bowl turning is so popular, especially given the speed with which a rough chunk of wood can be transformed into an object that can be used for decades and could easily survive centuries. In *Turned Bowl Design* (1985), I discussed what constitutes a good bowl. In this book, I concentrate on the *how* of making bowls: how I select wood, how I fix it on the lathe, how I use my gouges and scrapers to best advantage, how I sand and finish, and even how to price (should you wish to sell your work).

On the hardware side, there is information on the range of self-centering four-jaw chucks that have been developed since the mid 1980s to revolutionize the way we fix wood on the lathe. I show you how to get the best from these wonderful tools, which have become an essential lathe attachment.

In addition to all the chopping boards, plates, scoops, and some odd jobs I've done during my three decades as a professional woodturner, I've turned about 21,000 bowls, ranging from little 2-in. (50mm)-diameter salt bowls to one 28-in. (710mm)-diameter yew fruit bowl that I made on a borrowed lathe. Apart from that one, all my bowls have been less than 23¾ in. (600mm) diameter, which is the capacity of my lathe. About half have been from 6 in. to 12 in. diameter, nearly 2,800 more than 12 in. (305mm), and the rest smaller than 6 in. (150mm). I've turned bowls in a variety of ways, using all manner of cutting techniques and tools and a variety of faceplates, then chucks. I have always been looking for more fluency, convenience, and economy of effort so I can concentrate on the form rather than having to worry about technique. With all that comes speed and the ability to make the best use of your time, or even earn a living from the craft.

My aim is to provide you with a solid set of skills for turning bowls, whether you are just beginning or refining those techniques you have already. I describe the methods I employ using standard and readily available tools and equipment.

No matter what your level of expertise, you should gain something from this book because, with woodturning as with anything else, there are always ways to improve the status quo. And having found those ways, you'll need to practice them assiduously if you are to create the work of which you are capable.

My first bowl, seen in the top photo on p. 6, was 12 in. (305mm) in diameter and made of rippled ash. It took me 4½ hours to make and I expended a lot of nervous energy. Today it would take me well less than an hour and, I can guarantee, would be much better conceived and made. You might not feel pressured for time like a professional turning for a living, but learning how to make bowls efficiently will certainly increase your enjoyment of the craft.

Measurements are somewhat loose; even well-seasoned bowls have a habit of warping slightly or changing shape with changes in humidity, so I feel very precise measurements are pointless. For this reason, as well as for the sake of convenience, metric measurements have mostly been rounded to the nearest 5mm and imperial to ⅛ in.

Since the early 1980s, I have done quite a lot of teaching in "hands-on" workshops, and I have become very familiar with all the run-of-the-mill problems other turners typically experience when making bowls. (No surprise—they're the same that I had!) This book is structured so that when you have a problem, you can go to the section dealing with that stage of the bowl-making process and find out the probable cause and a definite solution.

Although I've made many delicate bowls that require handling like fine glass or porcelain, my main interest is in making utilitarian bowls that can be used for generations. This is not really a desire for some sort of immortality, although the idea of someone wondering who I might have been in a few hundred years as they gaze at my signature has its appeal. No, it's more an attitude of making things as well as possible so that they last. Wood is a resilient material that, if cared for, will last hundreds, if not thousands, of years. You might as well take advantage of its possibilities.

Finally, remember that craftsmanship has as much to do with knowing what to do when things go wrong as getting everything right all the time; that seldom happens. But the more experienced you become, the earlier you'll be able to spot impending problems and confidently overcome them. Only those who don't know will think there were no difficulties.

Richard Raffan
Canberra, Australia
August 2001

1 TURNING BOWLS: AN OVERVIEW

When you turn a wooden bowl, you are continuing a long tradition. Since the mid 1970s, woodturning has become a hugely popular hobby and a source of income for many. Competition among manufacturers catering to the burgeoning market means that there are now lathes, chucks, and tools that are infinitely superior to those of even 50 years ago. As a result, turning a bowl is a lot easier than it used to be. But making a good bowl, which is more than a hollow in a nice bit of well-finished wood, is just as challenging as it's always been. In this chapter, I'll set you on a path to making bowls that people will want to use and keep for generations.

A bowl is defined in dictionaries as a deep, round container for food and liquids that is open at the top. The word bowl comes from the Old English *bolla,* meaning root, indicating the long association between wood and bowls. For many centuries, most domestic tableware was turned from wood, and the common surname Turner reminds us that the craft was ubiquitous for generations. Sadly, hardly any wooden tableware has come down to us, presumably because it was tossed aside in favor of inexpensive china in the 19th century, when the industrial revolution made accessible all manner of things formerly the preserve of the wealthy.

The old wooden bowls that have survived are often well capable of several hundred years more use. There is no reason why, with a bit of

There is no reason why this 15-in. by 4¼-in. (380mm by 110mm) elm bowl I made in 1983 at a symposium in Ireland (and still one of my favorite bowls) should not have as long and useful a life as the 200-year-old Georgian table it's sitting on.

You should never let work you find unsatisfactory
out of the workshop—it will catch up with you eventually.

care and attention, any wooden bowl should not last every bit as long as a piece of antique furniture and certainly longer than anything ceramic.

These days common usage of the word bowl has broadened its meaning to include a host of quasi-utilitarian vessels made as purely decorative objects or artistic statements. Although I've turned my share of these, I like to think that just about every bowl I've made has at least one practical use as well as the ability to stand as a decorative object in its own right.

Attitude

Among the best and most appreciated bowls in my collection are several made by turners who have very little experience at the lathe. These people decided what they wanted to make and, undeterred by knowing little about the craft, set about doing it. Do such people have a manual in one hand while turning these immaculate pieces with the other? Each had a definite idea in mind and a determination to execute it that few of us seem to have. I am a great believer in people being able to achieve just about anything if they are interested enough and go about it carefully in the right way. It is depressing to meet turners who assume they cannot make a really good bowl because they are only amateurs. Amateurs have the time, unpressured by the need to earn a living. All that is required is desire and tenacity. Many of the best turned bowls I've seen over the past 30 years have been made by amateurs or part-time turners who do not rely on the craft for their livelihood.

Maple and stained oak, 3¼-in. and 3¾-in. (95mm and 83mm) diameter. Made in 1991 by Tore Olsson of Sweden.

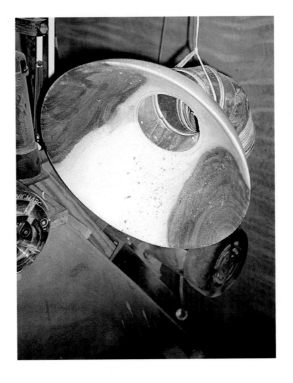

Al Gruntwagin of Florida didn't like the way his bowl was looking as a bowl, so he went through the base and made a dust-collection hood. The tall foot fits over the ducting and is pinned through the long grain.

The dramatic figure still visible in each of my first three bowls does not disguise the fact that these are dumpy pieces that are very heavy in the base.

The cross section, similar in each bowl, reveals a base that is too heavy. There are two linked, nearly flat sections instead of one flowing curve. The surface across the bottom of the inside is a very shallow V.

The characteristics of the wood or our own lack of technique often conspire to keep us from realizing our ideas, but try not to settle for second best. In Florida Al Gruntwagin didn't like the way his bowl was looking, but, not wanting his efforts to go to waste and having plenty of extra material in the foot to play with, he ended up with a fancy dust-collection hood (see the bottom photo on p. 5). Better a good dust hood than a bowl with unsatisfactory grain patterns.

If you are hoping to sell bowls for income, you should never let work you find unsatisfactory out of the workshop—it will catch up with you eventually. Nevertheless, you can regard every disaster or disappointment as a learning or design opportunity. If you go through the bottom of a thinner bowl, you have a potential lampshade. Splits can be detailed and bowls cut into pieces and reassembled. No matter if the resulting object is hideous; its creation and emergence should be fun and instructive, even if all you learn is that maybe you won't do that again.

Weight and Balance

It is very easy to rely on the glamour of the wood to make your bowl appealing. Turning a bowl that attracts attention is not difficult if the wood is flashy enough or if the defects and color are spectacular. But what is spectacular and shiny, or well finished and different, is not necessarily good, let alone a work of art.

All woods change color with age and exposure to sunlight. Logs or boards left exposed to the sun are bleached silver, while wood polished over the years with wax—or regular contact with sweaty palms—darkens and develops a shiny patina yet to be emulated synthetically.

Once the dramatic colors of flashy grain have faded, you are left with the form and balance of a bowl, and if this is not reasonably good, there is no reason why anyone should keep it. If a bowl is to survive generations, it needs a form that will enable it to stand as an appealing object even if painted matte black. The dramatic figure still visible in my first three bowls (see the top photo on the facing page) does not disguise the fact that these are dumpy pieces that are very heavy in the base. The bowl on the left has survived because it's the very first I made; otherwise I'd have re-turned it years ago (and I might do so yet). My fourth bowl, the one shown in the bottom photo on the facing page, was not so lucky; my mother used it for about 15 years before I cut it in half, as a fine example of the sort of mediocre bowl I hope to prevent people from making.

These early bowls of mine are highly functional, but they don't look too good compared with their more considered stablemates pictured elsewhere in this book. Their profiles are dumpy, but their main shortcoming is that when handled they are very unbalanced—their tapering rims, less than flowing curves, and heavy bases don't feel good in the hand. In the afterword, I will suggest ways the tactile qualities of such bowls can be rectified by redistributing the weight within the form, so that there is a better balance between the base and the rim.

Early bowls typically are somewhat heavy, partly because few of us want to push our luck

and ruin hours of work with one cut too many. But it's also easy to get so carried away with the techniques that you create a profile with several facets, heavy beads, and other bits of turned frippery. This raises the problem of what you might do with the inside of such a form. Sort-of-round-it-out is the usual response, and of course sort-of-rounded-out is how it will look. A better approach is to keep the profile relatively

There was a time when I made hundreds of impractical bowls like these, and it's worth making a few for the wonderful been-there-done-that feeling.

Bowls with a small foot can be very elegant, but the walnut one (left) needs pebbles inside to keep it upright. The laburnum (right) is far more practical and looks and feels better when handled.

simple, especially at first. You'll have enough to keep you busy cutting nice flowing curves, let alone sanding and finishing them.

When you pick up a bowl, it needs to feel right in your hand, and being well balanced is an important part of that. Having the weight in the bottom of the bowl can work well when the wall tapers to the rim. In such a form you expect the weight to be towards the base; if it isn't, then practical and physical repercussions, as well as aesthetic liabilities, ensue. The elm bowl shown in the top photo on p. 7, with its thin, even wall, might be a technical achievement, but such bowls can look as though they've been molded. And ultra-lightweight pieces need to be kept in a draft-free environment or weighted down. In the late 1970s I made hundreds of thin bowls, but I got over the obsession once I realized how impractical they are and knew I could do it. But it's still worth making a few, for that wonderful been-there-done-that feeling.

A bowl with a very small foot, as shown at left in the bottom photo on p. 7, can be very elegant, though rather impractical; this one needs some weight in it to keep it upright.

Curves

As a woodturner, you are always working with curved surfaces, and the moment you move away from cylinders and cones you have the curve of the profile to consider. Cylindrical and conical surfaces are so definable and easy to check with a straightedge that I prefer to avoid them. And you don't get many straight lines in the natural world. Curves are more provocative and varied, which is why, when they are just right, they can lift a familiar form from good to sublime.

At its simplest, a curve is a bent line that is devoid of flat sections, bumps, and dips. This seems simple enough, but in fact curves like this are rare in the turned bowls you see in street markets, stores, or even galleries. Many get very near, but many more, like the inside shown in the bottom photo on p. 6, don't. A curve doesn't change direction abruptly. Take as an example a smooth curve of a circle, where the line bends continuously and evenly to meet up with itself. But even a small section of such an even curve tends to be rather uninteresting or too formal when applied to a turned bowl. Asymmetric curves like the portion of a spiral or the catenary curves of the hanging chain shown in the photo on the facing page have far more appeal.

As work proceeds, you can watch a curve develop on the upper horizon of a bowl. But only when you stop the lathe and run your hand over the surface can you begin to appreciate its qualities. Even then, it can be difficult to ascertain whether your curve really flows in one smooth trajectory. A quick pass with fine 240-grit abrasive instantly reveals the major deviations as it smoothes the high spots, highlighting those portions of the developing curve that need attention. Most often, even small deviations on the line of a curve must be turned away. Abrasives smooth what's there.

Knowing when a curve needs slight alteration or an adjustment of proportions, or when enough is enough, comes only with experience. But by assessing the images that assail the eyes and stimulate the brain on a continuous basis,

Even small deviations on the line of a curve
must be turned away. Abrasives smooth what's there.

you can develop your eye for form. Analyze why you like some curves, forms, or proportions over others. This is especially useful when comparing similar everyday objects around you. Why does the shape of one motor vehicle appeal more than another, or one desk lamp, or ceramic vase. If you can feel the curves, that's even better, since this develops your sense of touch.

As Work Proceeds

It is said to be better to travel hopefully than to arrive, but with a lump of diminishing wood, a destination is no bad thing. When you fix a blank on the lathe, you need a vague idea of the form you are going to make. Aim to travel in the right direction with the intention of stopping when things look about right. I work assuming that what can go wrong will go wrong, so I never do anything until absolutely necessary. The shape of the blank I begin with and the form I'm intending to make dictate the ways I go about turning a bowl, but at each stage, whenever possible, I allow a margin for error. When there are difficult cuts looming, I take the opportunity to practice during the roughing stages, when a catch won't matter so much.

Turning a basic, usable bowl is not difficult, and there are many ways of going about it. You could hold the bowl by the base and turn it in one go, but that's rarely done. If you hold the blank by what will be the top of the bowl you can turn the profile from any direction, and if some flaw emerges like a hole behind a bit of bark or a hidden knot, you can turn it away or do something with it. Defects discovered later, when hollowing is nearly complete, are usually a problem and difficult to incorporate into the bowl.

If you need to alter the proportions after turning the profile, it's easy to remove some of the base. But if the bowl is gripped by the base, there is no simple way to reduce the diameter of the base, and if you reduce the height by turn-

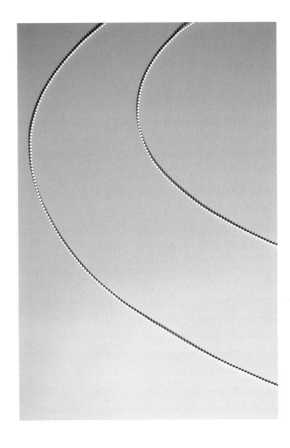

Any section of a catenary curve, the kind of curve formed by a chain hanging from two points, can be applied satisfactorily to a bowl profile.

ing away the rim, you can often simultaneously shrink the diameter of the bowl.

For years before the introduction of the self-centering four-jaw chucks that revolutionized the way we can hold wood on the lathe, I followed the then standard practice of mounting on a faceplate twice. First I oriented the blank so that what would become the top of the bowl was toward the faceplate, and I roughed out the bowl's profile. Then I remounted the blank the other way around, in order to hollow the inside and complete the outside. The disadvantage of working this way is that the screw holes remain in the base, although I became adept at filling these so they were almost invisible. More of a problem was hitting one or more of the screws as I completed the internal sweep of the bowl, but I learned to resharpen my tools and make those holes look like knots. I could have left the base thicker to accommodate the mounting screws and turned away the screw holes by reverse-mounting, but that wasted a lot of wood and took time with little financial gain. So I reserved that technique for exhibition pieces.

Today it is still common practice to start by gripping a bowl blank on what will be the top of the bowl. But after that just about everything can be done using a chuck to hold the bowl in its various stages of development, provided there is a true surface for it to grip. There are times when you might rechuck a bowl several times in quick succession, but any inconvenience is eclipsed by the ability to keep your design options open longer and the better access for the tools.

Modern self-centering four-jaw chucks have many accessory jaw sets that enable you to grip a series of diameters barely marring the wood, either contracting around a foot or expanding into a recess, which enables you to take a bowl from the chuck completely finished. In addition, as work proceeds, you can take a bowl on and off the lathe as often as you like to check its weight and balance and generally see how it's developing. Yet another advantage is that they allow you to retain some method of holding a bowl in the finished piece so that, at a later date, it can easily be remounted and refurbished. Many finishes deteriorate drastically after a few years, and refurbishing off the lathe is often so difficult that the bowls are discarded.

Basic Tool Handling

The basic cuts required to turn bowls are relatively easy to master, especially compared with those for spindles or hollowing end grain. Bowl-turning gouges aren't as intimidating as skew chisels, but the catches (when the edge is snapped onto the rest with a bang) that terrify many a novice remain an ever-present possibility. Most of the problems encountered by woodturners on both lathe and grinder result from a bull-in-a-china-shop, when-in-doubt-use-force approach. On a high-speed grinder, this makes

for a dull but colorful blue and gold edge, while at the lathe any force combined with a blunt tool soon leads to a general lack of control and the edge catching.

There are two important points to remember at all times working on a lathe. The first is that if you let the wood bear down on an unsupported edge, that edge will catch. If you put the tool on the wood before the rest, as shown Figure 1 in the illustration on the facing page, there is nothing to prevent it being smacked onto the rest. Whenever there is space between the tool edge and the rest, the tool will roll to fill the gap.

In the context of gouges, it is very important to appreciate the difference between a deep-fluted and a shallow gouge. Deep-fluted gouges can be used flute up because the bevel rides the wood and supports the edge, as shown in Figure 2 in the illustration on the facing page. A shallow gouge is never used flute up when turning a bowl because any downward force snaps the tool over as shown in Figure 3 in the illustration on the facing page. Photos will remind you of this throughout the book.

Second, let the wood come to the tool. You don't need to push the edge into the wood like a woodcarver. Let the lathe do the hard work of spinning the wood, bringing it to the edge. All you need do is hold the tool edge in the optimum position to slice the wood as it passes, and move the tool forward only as fast as the wood reaches the edge.

Sound is an important diagnostic tool. If a blank has a split, a loose knot, a defect, or is uneven, there's a characteristic tick-tick sound. Thin wood starts to vibrate, especially if you are pushing the tool against a thin bowl wall, and the result is a range of brittle and screeching sounds, the intensity of which depends on the thinness of the wood and the pressure being applied. The wood doesn't like being tortured, so if it starts screaming it's kinder to stop and ascertain the cause. If the base becomes thin, there'll be a hollow sound like a xylophone or

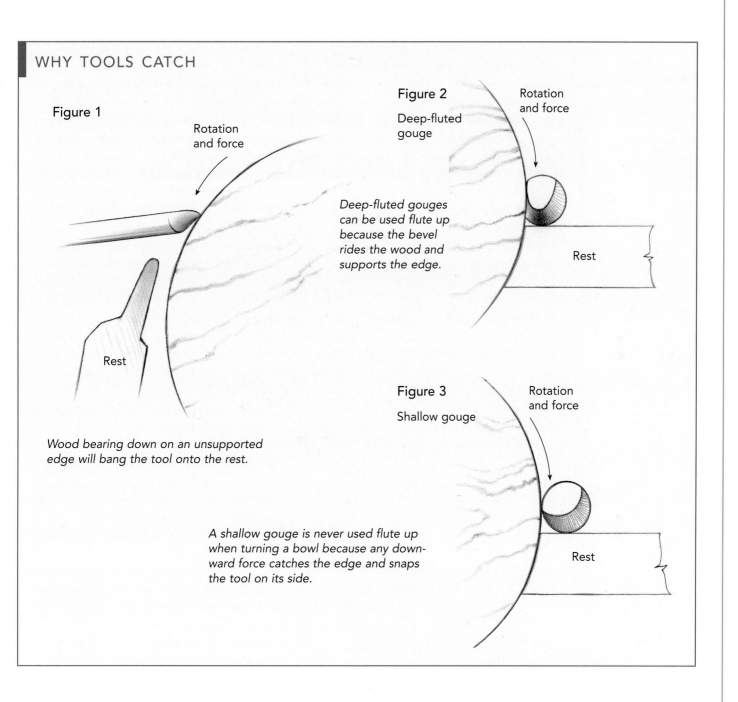

WHY TOOLS CATCH

Figure 1

Rotation and force

Rest

Wood bearing down on an unsupported edge will bang the tool onto the rest.

Figure 2

Deep-fluted gouge

Rotation and force

Rest

Deep-fluted gouges can be used flute up because the bevel rides the wood and supports the edge.

Figure 3

Shallow gouge

Rotation and force

Rest

A shallow gouge is never used flute up when turning a bowl because any downward force catches the edge and snaps the tool on its side.

Sound is an important diagnostic tool.
If a blank has a split, a loose knot, a defect, or is uneven,
there's a characteristic tick-tick sound.

marimba. If you keep turning, the base will become really thin and springy enough to flex when pushed.

If the wood doesn't spin when you switch on the lathe and there's a loud screech, you have the drive spindle locked and the belt is slipping on the pulleys.

Whenever you hear a sound that you don't recognize on the lathe, it is essential that you stop work, cut the power instantly, and determine the source of the new noise. For a novice this is a time-consuming business, but you soon build a vast library of sounds in your mind and learn which are friendly and which are not. A change in the pitch of any sound on the lathe is often a warning that something is not as it should be. Remember that when things go wrong on a lathe they go wrong fast and that lumps of flying wood can do a lot of damage to you, windows, and anything else in the firing line.

For the first couple of years, I turned all my bowls from 3-in.- to 6-in.- (75mm to 150mm) thick air-dried lumber, which in the early 1970s was still readily available. Climbing around the seasoned stacks in a sawmiller's drying sheds and picking out boards was always an enjoyable day out. Then in 1973, I couldn't find enough suitable dry timber for a large order, and I was forced to turn freshly sawn lumber into rough-turned bowls for rapid drying in a kiln. That was something of a disaster (they mostly split), but the whole experience led me to rethink the way I made bowls.

Since 1973 I have rough-turned all my bowls in green wood, making thick versions of the final shape. I set them aside to air-dry, then remount them on the lathe for final shaping and finishing some months or years later. Although I worked this out for myself, I later learned that this methodology has long been standard practice for commercial bowl turners in other parts of the world, including a Japanese bowl turner I visited in 1992.

Practice

If you are entirely new to bowl turning, you will be itching to complete a few to impress your family and friends and justify the investment in lathe, tools, and wood. Get some dry wood or blanks for your first few bowls. After that I urge novice bowl turners to rough-turn a quantity of bowls before returning to finish them. You rough out the bowls from freshly felled timber, set them aside to dry, then after a few months remount them on the lathe to be trued-up and completed. The bowls will warp somewhat as they dry, but they rarely split except around knots or particularly stressed area of grain; I reckon my losses due to splitting at less than five percent. Rough-turning enables you to get the maximum from green logs that would otherwise split if left solid. A small tree—say 12 in. (305mm) in diameter—should yield bowls about 1 in. (25mm) less in diameter. Similarly, dimensioned defect-free seasoned wood would likely come from a tree nearly twice that diameter.

Roughing out bowls provides wonderful practice, and turning green wood ranges from highly enjoyable to exhilarating. Thick, wide shavings arc from the tool edge to a pile on the

Tasmanian myrtle, 9 in. by 3¾ in. (230mm by 95mm). Finished when the wood was partly seasoned, this bowl warped slightly as I hoped. In more than 10 years of daily use as a food bowl, the bowl has darkened from its original light pink and become very smooth. The rounded and slightly thicker base allows it to wobble slightly but not tip over.

floor while the form appears as if by magic. If the wood is as freshly felled as recommended, you can get so wet from the sap flying out that you might find full wet-weather gear useful. But the real bonus will be that when you come to complete the seasoned bowls, you'll be able to proceed with a good deal more confidence. Partly seasoned bowls also can be completed, and if they warp a bit like the salad bowl shown in the photo on the facing page, which is used daily, so what? I rounded the base to allow for this.

Support and Advice

I have always worked alone and mostly enjoyed it. The only real drawback when you start out is assessing how well you might be progressing. I started my turning life in a small country workshop where during the cleanup each day I could poke around master turner Rendle Crang's lathe and see the sort of mess I should be making from which tools. I soon learned that not all woods are capable of producing those long spiral shavings that are a major attraction of woodturning and that different woods produce a different type of shaving depending on the grain structure within the timber (see the photo on p. 15).

It's handy, too, to have people whose judgement you trust with whom to discuss what you're doing, whether in terms of technique or design. I was fortunate to know a number of very good professional artist/craftsman potters and furniture makers when I started turning. These individuals were prepared to discuss all the aspects of design and making that constitute craftsmanship. Admiring friends and relatives might be good for the ego, as are sales, but rarely does either help to develop the overall quality of your work.

Maximum Speeds for Bowl Turning

Speeds for rough-turning blanks should be approximately half those shown. The exact speeds at which a blank can be safely spun depends on its density and balance. Always err on the side of caution and select a low speed when first spinning a blank on the lathe. If you have a variable-speed lathe, always start from near zero.

DIAMETER	HEIGHT				
	2 in. (50mm)	3 in. (75mm)	4 in. (100mm)	5 in. (125mm)	6 in. (150mm)
4 in. (100mm)	1,800*	1,600	1,500	1,400	1,300
6 in. (150mm)	1,600	1,500	1,400	1,300	1,100
8 in. (200mm)	1,500	1,400	1,300	1,100	1,200
10 in. (250mm)	1,400	1,300	1,100	1,200	1,000
12 in. (305mm)	1,300	1,100	1,200	1,000	800
14 in. (355mm)	1,100	1,100	1,000	800	600
16 in. (410mm)	1,100	1,000	800	600	500

*The figures in this chart are expressed in rpm.

SAFETY AROUND THE LATHE

You can have a very serious accident working on a lathe, and if you doubt this, compare insurance quotes for woodturning against almost any other occupation. The wood is spinning fast and can be off balance. If the lathe is switched on at too high a speed for the blank, the blank will fly off and could kill you. Besides all this, you are dealing with sharp tools (or the sometimes more hazardous dull ones).

The risks are real and can't be overemphasized. It's easy to become complacent and careless, especially when you think you have a machine and techniques under control. So, as you approach the lathe or any other machine, always hesitate a second to remind yourself that it is potentially dangerous. Always think about what you are about to do and advance with care from the right direction. Here are some specific safety precautions to keep in mind and incorporate into your routine.

1. Always check the lathe and work area before you begin. Check that any guards are in place and secure, that no wrenches or keys are left in shafts or chucks, and that no tools or materials will interfere with the lathe's operation. A quick visual examination should become a regular work habit.

2. Check that speeds are set correctly for the work you are about to do.

3. Wear a face shield, and remember to put the visor down. It's there to protect your face and fend off shavings, not catch them. With the shield in place, you are less likely to require cosmetic surgery when a block flies off the lathe and hits you in the face (as it will). Over the years I've had four lots of stitches mending my face and forehead, not to mention a big hole in my left forearm.

4. Always remove chuck keys or locking bars from any chuck on the lathe when you are not actually using them. There have been a lot of very serious injuries sustained by flying chuck keys and tommy bars.

5. Before starting the lathe, rotate the wood by hand to see that it revolves freely. Check that the tool rest is immobile, with all locking levers tightened.

6. Stand clear of the firing line of the lathe when switching it on because blocks are bound to come off now and then. When an object comes off the lathe, it usually travels at 90 degrees to the axis.

7. Never wrap a polishing cloth, sandpaper, steel wool, or anything else around your hands or fingers. Spinning wood or the lathe can grab these in a fraction of a second, and it's not worth being attached to the other end and risking a finger.

8. Stop the lathe before adjusting the rest. If you move the rest carelessly and it makes contact with the rotating work, you are likely to damage the work or jar it from the lathe. You might even shatter delicate or fragile jobs. In any case, your hands will be perilously close to the action.

9　Beware of sharp edges, corners, and rims on the work. Razor-sharp edges can develop rapidly and are just as efficient as bacon slicers in cutting you to the bone—often without pain but with a lot of blood (and that stains the wood). Develop the habit of softening edges either with coarse abrasives or a tool.

10　Never lean over machines, even when switched off: They might suddenly leap into action and grab you or your clothing.

11　Never wear loose clothing. Short sleeves are best, but long sleeves with elastic cuffs are an acceptable option.

12　Do not allow ties, chains, or pendants around the neck to hang free. Remove them or tuck them away.

13　If your hair is long, tie it back. Or, even better, stick it under a hat and keep the dust off as well. If you do a lot of turning and wear a long beard, you are gambling with the odds. (It has happened.)

14　Remove all jewelry and watches from your hands and wrists. They might catch or simply be worn away when you are sanding.

15　Keep your fingernails cut short so they are less likely to catch on the work or chucks.

16　Wear shoes or strapped sandals rather than slip-ons.

17　Keep the floor clear of loose cables, blocks of wood, and such.

18　Store solvents, finishes, and steel wool away from any potential sparks and particularly from the grinder. All these are combustible.

Same cuts, different woods. When learning what kind of mess you should be making, know that some woods leave the tool as long spirals while others, like the pinkish jarrah burl chips in front, do not.

These days there are lots of woodturning clubs across the English-speaking world where you can find fellow turners with whom to communicate, and there are major woodturning symposiums that cover the full range of activities pertaining to the lathe, including design and marketing. You'll find these very stimulating and advertised in the woodworking press and on the Internet.

The downside of woodturning groups is that they tend to be preoccupied with wood and finishes and not so concerned with the design, form, and function, which in the long term are even more important aspects of a finished bowl. Curiously, comparatively few woodturners have an arts background or, in my experience, even an interest in the arts. This is in contrast to most potters and glass-blowers, who also spin their raw material into objects. It is worth looking closely at all manner of craft work, especially when it's possible to discern the hand of a particular maker. A personal style will develop unless you rigorously control your work, and it's always a useful exercise to study why two apparently similar objects differ in their appeal.

2 TOOLS FOR TURNING BOWLS

This chapter deals with the equipment you need to turn bowls. First I'll discuss lathes suited to turning bowls, suggesting what to look for or avoid in each of the major components that make up a lathe. You'll find advice on purchasing a lathe for bowl turning, but if such an acquisition is financially out of reach, I'll suggest how you can build your own. Finally, there is a section on tools, chucks, and the ancillary equipment such as drills, dust extractors, and the saws that enable you to prepare your raw material.

Lathes

A lathe is a simple device that spins materials—in our case wood—around a horizontal axis and against a cutting tool. Over the centuries lathes have been universally adapted to produce zillions of round objects in every material imaginable in hundreds of trades. All varieties of lathe, whether powered by hand, foot, waterwheel, or electricity, have variations of the same basic components.

Wood lathes are manufactured with either a long or short bed, with the headstock to the left and tailstock to the right as shown in the photo at left. You can turn bowls on any of them, but it's a right-handed world, to which left-handers must adapt if the bed is long. However, because bowls are rarely even 12 in. (305mm) high, you don't need a long bed, so bowl lathes generally have a short bed, which allows you to move across the axis when hollowing enclosed forms (see chapter 5).

The maximum diameter that can be turned, or swung, on a lathe is determined by the height of the center above the bed. A lathe with a center height of 8 in. (200mm) will swing 16 in. (400mm).

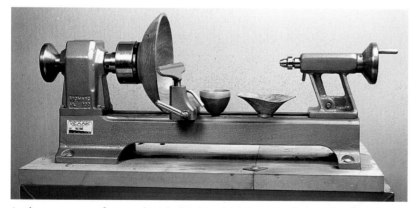

Lathes are manufactured with the headstock to the left and tailstock to the right. On this sturdy little lathe, you can turn bowls up to 9 in. (230mm) in diameter.

THE LATHE

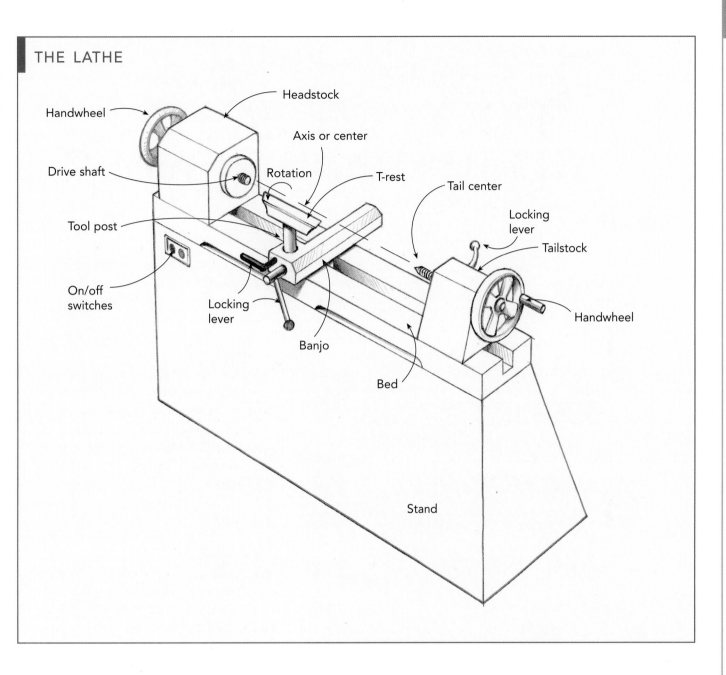

Handwheel

Headstock

Axis or center

Drive shaft

Rotation

T-rest

Tail center

Tool post

Locking lever

Tailstock

On/off switches

Locking lever

Banjo

Bed

Handwheel

Stand

Wood frequently varies in density, with heartwood typically harder and denser than the sapwood. If you spin material of varying density at high speed, it will vibrate, so the components of the lathe need to be substantial enough to limit vibration. In theory, lathes can never be heavy enough.

I turn bowls on one of my two Vicmarc 300 lathes. Similar to several lathes commercially available, including the Woodfast and Oneway, these have an electronic variable-speed control and will swing 23½ in. (600mm), allowing me to make bowls that are far larger than most domestic situations can easily accommodate. Bowls larger than 14 in. (355mm) in diameter overwhelm most dining tables, and the large chunks of wood needed to make them are increasingly difficult to obtain. These machines

A BOWL TURNER'S WORKSPACE

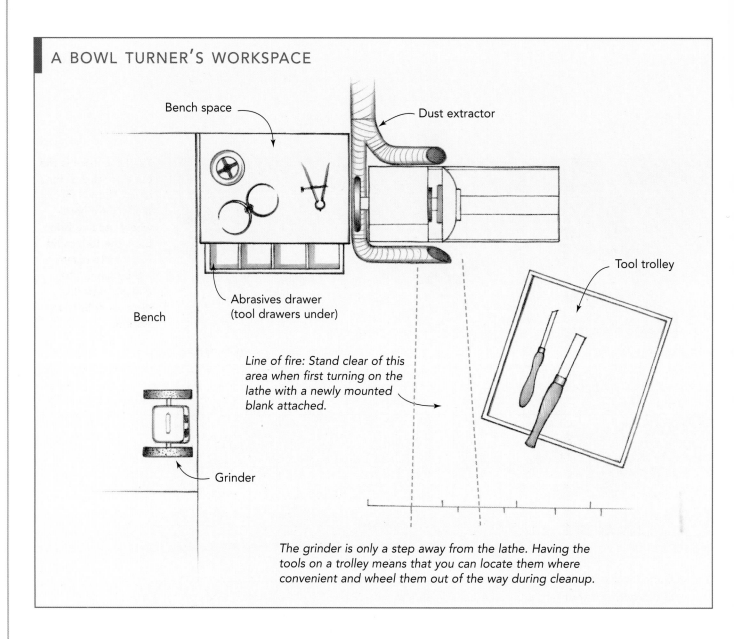

Bench space

Dust extractor

Tool trolley

Abrasives drawer
(tool drawers under)

Bench

*Line of fire: Stand clear of this
area when first turning on the
lathe with a newly mounted
blank attached.*

Grinder

*The grinder is only a step away from the lathe. Having the
tools on a trolley means that you can locate them where
convenient and wheel them out of the way during cleanup.*

are overkill for most amateur turners and prob-ably of a capacity rarely used to the fullest by most professionals.

THE HEADSTOCK

The headstock houses the drive shaft through which power is transmitted to the wood. I like a drive shaft 1¼ in. (30mm) in diameter, mount-ed in ball or tapered-roller bearings that are 3 in. (75mm) to 4 in. (100mm) in diameter. When powered by a 1-hp motor, this combina-tion of drive shaft and bearings will easily han-dle a 75-lb. (34kg) block of wood. More impor-tantly, while this combination copes with the stresses involved when spinning the off-balance chunks of wood from which most of the best grain patterns come, it gains full speed in a few seconds and can be stopped as quickly.

A shaft larger than 1½ in. (38mm) or 2 in. (50mm) in diameter will be much heavier, requiring larger bearings and motor (2 hp to 3 hp), all of which make it much slower to start

The maximum diameter that can be turned on a lathe is determined by the height of the center above the bed.

The headstock is the business end of the lathe. The wheel to the left is a handwheel used to bring the lathe to a rapid halt and to rotate a job by hand. The ducting is part of the dust-collection system.

and stop and involve a higher energy cost. But it is worth considering if your interest is turning deep bowls in excess of 24 in. (610mm) in diameter.

If your interest is in bowls less than 12 in. (305mm) in diameter, you can get by with a lighter-weight drive shaft, but the smallest I would consider using is 1 in. (25mm) in diameter, mounted in 3-in. (75mm) bearings. Anything smaller, commonly fitted on low-price lathes, is rarely satisfactory and not up to coping with the stresses involved in turning bowls, especially when mounted in solid bronze bearings.

Even if small, both drive shaft and bearings should be mounted in a heavy casing, ideally of cast iron. There should be no play in the bearings because any play will be magnified at the point where the tool is cutting. Not only does this make fine work impossible, but it also leads to dangerous vibration and tool catches. If the drive shaft is not seated properly in the bearings or if the bearings become worn, the lathe will knock or whine as it runs. When this occurs, the bearings must be adjusted or replaced to ensure safety.

On any lathe it's handy to have a hollow drive shaft machined to accept a Morse-taper drive. Although Morse-taper drives are rarely

An easily reached locking pin is essential for locking the shaft when removing chucks.

A swivel headstock makes many hollowing cuts easier and also enables you to turn larger work than is possible over the bed. A tool post that goes to the floor helps minimize vibration.

used by bowl turners, a hollow shaft is also handy for setting up a vacuum chuck (see pp. 154–155). A drive shaft should be threaded at both ends to accept faceplates and chucks. On the outboard thread (left of the headstock), you should have a handwheel, or a faceplate that can be used as a handwheel, as shown in photos on p. 19. A handwheel, while not essential, makes life a whole lot easier because it enables you to bring the lathe rapidly to a stop. And it's handy for rotating a job by hand (with the lathe off) so you can inspect work in progress.

If you're left-handed, you might consider working outboard, although all the lefties I've met work inboard, and also right-handed when left-handed techniques are impossible.

The threads on the outboard end of the drive shaft must be opposite to those inboard, so that chucks and faceplates will screw on against the machine's rotation.

If lathes have a reversing switch to aid sanding and finishing, look for a way to lock chucks and faceplates on the spindle. If there is none, you'll need to ensure that any chuck or faceplate doesn't unscrew as you start the lathe in reverse. Try spinning the work by hand as you press the start button to overcome the inertia that causes a chuck or faceplate to unwind.

You must be able to lock the drive shaft to remove chucks and faceplates easily. A wrench on a flat or octagonal section of the shaft is best, but most manufacturers now opt for a pin that slots into the drive shaft or largest pulley, often doubling as an indexing head (see the top photo at left). An indexing head allows you to set the lathe in a number of positions at regular intervals for applying decorative patterns to your bowls.

SWIVEL HEADSTOCKS

Some headstocks with integral motors can be rotated to allow you to swing large diameters, unrestricted by the lathe bed (see the bottom photo on the facing page). The advantage of these headstocks is that many hollowing cuts are easier, particularly on enclosed forms. And you also have a centerwork lathe should you need it. But of course you can't use the tail center when the headstock is rotated. Tail-center support can be handy for security during some finishing techniques and essential in others (see p. 151). To keep vibration within acceptable limits, swivel headstocks need to be substantial, as does the rest of the lathe.

A swivel headstock was a feature of my first Coronet Major lathe. It sounds like a nice option since it gives you better access to the job, but I've never found this arrangement satisfactory unless the rests are supported from the floor. If you have a swivel-head lathe with a bed bolted to the headstock but no support from the floor, consider supporting the rest using lengths of timber wedged between the rest assembly and the floor, or installing a long tool post, as shown in the bottom photo on the facing page.

THE TAILSTOCK

For years I turned on Harrison Graduate short-bed bowl lathes. They served me well and I made thousands of bowls on them, mostly without the aid of the tail center, which was tedious to set up and remove as well as inaccurate. You can manage without a tail center, but there are many techniques where it will make life a whole lot easier. If you are going to have a tail center, it might as well be a good one, similar to that shown in the photo at right.

The tailstock houses a center that is mounted in a threaded spindle: You lock the tailstock in a convenient position on the lathe bed, then wind in the center to support the job. The locking mechanism needs to be quick and effective. A locking lever that remains attached to the assembly is better than a nut and separate wrench, which can get lost in shavings.

A tailstock needs to be solid and accurately aligned with the headstock and lathe axis.

Normally, you want the tailstock well out of the way while turning a bowl. You can locate it at the end of a long bed if the bed is long enough, as I do on my long-bed lathe. On a short-bed lathe, it's simpler to remove it altogether. Although heavy, my Vicmarc tailstock is easy to slide on and off the short-bed lathe. But in order to avoid bending and lifting, I store the tailstock at much the same level, either on my spare lathe or a holder on a nearby bench specifically made for that purpose.

A handwheel is used to wind the tail center in and out, and a locking lever should keep it in place once adjusted. Look for an adjustment range of at least 4 in. (100mm), which will give you room to work around a bowl and save having to move the whole assembly if you are popping a bowl in and out of a chuck with tail support, as discussed on p. 152.

The tail center needs to be absolutely in line with the headstock axis, otherwise it will loosen work mounted on a chuck or faceplate rather

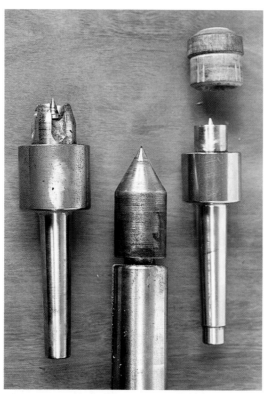

Revolving tail centers come in various shapes. The cone center (center) penetrates the wood more than the cup centers (left and right). The turned wooden flat center (top right) fits over the cup center shown below it, keeping the center from marking the wood.

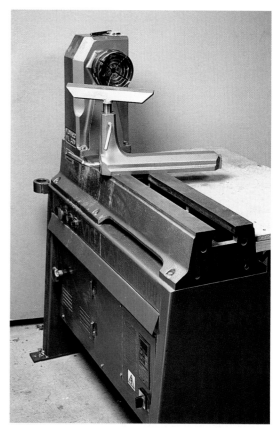

Ideally a lathe should be made of cast iron on a heavy stand, here constructed of ³⁄₁₆-in. (5mm) sheet steel. This lathe weighs about 396 lb. (180kg).

than keep it in place. To check the alignment of a center, mount and true up a bowl blank on the lathe. Then clamp the tailstock firmly in place and wind in the tail center against the spinning wood so that it just touches the surface. If the center is inaccurately aligned, it will mark a circle on the wood; if accurate, a cone. Some lathes have set screws that enable you to make adjustments. If the center is low and to one side, use shims between the tailstock and the lathe bed to realign it. Often a sheet of folded paper will be sufficient. If the center is too high, there's little you can do except sand or remachine the underside of the tailstock.

Most lathes come with a dead or cup center made of solid metal. These need lubrication

(traditionally animal fat, but these days oil) on the work itself to prevent the support from loosening through friction burning. A better option is a revolving tail center. I use conical and cup centers, plus a flat wooden center I turned to fit over one of the cup centers, as shown in the photo at left above. The wooden insert keeps the cup center from marring the wood.

THE BED AND STAND

The best headstock, tailstock, and rests are rendered next to useless unless mounted on a heavily constructed bed supported by an equally substantial stand. A solid and well-built lathe similar to that shown in the photo at right above will

The lathe bed should be thick-section cast iron,

which absorbs vibration better than steel bars or extruded aluminum.

eliminate troublesome vibration and make turning much easier and safer.

Ideally, the bed should be thick-section cast iron, which absorbs vibration better than the steel bars or extruded aluminum sections found on less-expensive lathes. Most good-quality lathes have a cast-iron bed supported by a stand made of 3/16-in. (5mm) sheet steel or heavy angle iron, each of which can provide excellent rigid support.

The stand, in addition to being heavy, needs to have as wide a footprint as possible. Most of the best lathes have stands that are at least twice the width of the lathe bed, similar to the Vicmarc 300 in the photo at right on the facing page.

Many good small lathes are sold on lightweight stands, which must be either strengthened or replaced. A good solution, if you have a floor that can take the strain and don't intend to move the lathe too often, is to mount your lathe on a big lump of concrete or bench filled with sand.

SWITCHES AND MOTORS

You must be able to switch the lathe off instantly if something goes wrong. The best arrangement is a long switch-off bar like that shown in the photos at right on the facing page and at right. Accessible from various work positions, the bar needs to be pressed only lightly to cut the power. More common, the red "off" button on the magnetic switch alone is also activated by a light touch.

Make sure that the switch is located on the front of the lathe where you can reach it easily, not tucked into some corner or on the far side of the lathe bed. You should be able to cut the

Electronic on/off switches are essential for safety. You can cut the power instantly by touching the red button. In addition, the red bar that runs the length of the lathe requires only a nudge to cut the power.

power by leaning against the off switch while your hands are otherwise occupied.

Some manufacturers offer a movable switch that can be kept close to where you're working. I prefer to keep the switch located in one place so I know where it is; if things go wrong, you don't always have time to remember where you placed it. Having linked switches at either end of the lathe is a good idea; this way you don't have to cross the line of fire to turn off the lathe (see the illustration on p. 18).

Before the introduction of electronic variable-speed motors, each of my lathes was powered by a single-phase 1-hp electric motor that provided more than enough power to rotate blanks up to 75 lb. (34kg). Most electronic variable-speed systems employ 1½-hp motors. On smaller lathes swinging less than 10 in. (250mm), a ½-hp motor is sufficient.

SPEEDS AND VARIABLE-SPEED SYSTEMS

Bowl turning often requires that you adjust the lathe speed because you need low speeds to rough-down an off-balance blank, then progressively higher speeds as work proceeds. Speeds need to be easy to adjust, so where it's required that you manually reposition a drive belt on pulleys, you want the drive belts, pulleys, and tensioning devices readily accessible.

A bowl lathe should have speeds ranging from about 350 rpm to 2,000 rpm maximum, and the more options you have, the better. A six-step pulley will give you more flexibility than a four-step one. The upper range is used only for small bowls. When setting speeds, it's better to try a slower speed first than to discover you have a blank spinning too fast (see the speed chart on p. 13).

Step pulleys provide a limited number of speeds. A better (though more expensive) option is a variable-speed control, which allows you to select exactly the speed you want. These transmissions can be mechanical or electronic. Mechanical systems use floating or sprung pulleys, which enable you to vary the speed by moving a lever that gradually changes the relative diameter of the pulleys.

Mechanical speed controls work well enough, although loss of torque can be a problem and they tend to be fairly noisy compared with electronic systems. A major disadvantage is that speeds can be adjusted only with the lathe running. You soon remember to work around this once you've mounted a large blank and forgotten to select a low speed a few times because you have to remove the blank, start the lathe, lower the speed, then remount your blank—all of which is an irritating waste of time.

Should things go wrong with a mechanical speed control, tweaking or repair is easy; an electronic variable-speed control is a different matter. Like most of us, I'd need an electronics whiz to fix one, which usually means extracting the motor and switches from the lathe and sending them away for a few minutes work. Fortunately the electronics are now very reliable, but as a professional turner who in the past has spent hours taking speed controls in and out of lathes (not my current lathes), I still retain my old mechanical variable-speed lathe for emergencies.

There can be problems bringing a lathe to a rapid stop with some electronic speed controls. Those that have electronic braking allow you to set the time in which the lathe will slow to a stop. But once you program the stopping speed, you cannot stop the lathe any faster, even by gripping the handwheel. This can be dangerous if a turning comes loose on the lathe or jams, as frequently happens when nesting bowls. You have to be able to stop the lathe instantly when things go wrong.

If the lathe is programmed to stop in a set time, say five seconds or more, waiting for it to stop can be very frustrating. I stop the lathe frequently to examine work in progress. I typically bring the lathe to a halt within two seconds using the handwheel, so waiting another two or three seconds breaks into the rhythm of work and loses me a good deal of time in the long run.

An electronic brake can be set to stop the lathe in a second, but this raises another problem. If you stop the lathe too quickly, inertia keeps heavy chucks, and the chunks of wood they hold, spinning, causing them to unwind from the spindle. This is also dangerous. Never attempt to catch a spinning chuck if it comes off the lathe. Usually it will drop onto the lathe bed, but it might bounce onto the floor at 90 degrees to the lathe bed, in which case you need to get out of the way fast. Electronic braking requires a compromise: For blanks less than 12 in. (305mm) in diameter, set the stopping speed at around three seconds, and you will avoid most of the problems of stopping too quickly and unwinding chucks, while minimizing the dangers and inefficiencies of stopping too slowly. For larger work, set the stopping speed at five seconds or more.

Electronic variable-speed controls typically allow you to vary the speed from zero to as high as 3,000 rpm. Mostly for reasons of torque, electronic variable-speed systems usually operate on step pulleys with two or three steps. For heavier work, always set the drive belt to the low-speed range and consequently a low maximum speed. With this comes an important safety advantage because, in the low range, you cannot spin the wood at dangerously high speeds.

If you always work in high range, it is easy to inadvertently turn the lathe on at too high a speed for the wood mounted. For example, if you've been turning a small bowl at 2,000 rpm, it's easy to forget to lower the speed if you then mount a 14-in. (355mm)-diameter blank on the lathe. If you forget to change the speed and spin a large blank at high rpm, the blank can explode, fly off the lathe, or rattle the lathe to bits—all dangerous eventualities I've experienced and witnessed a number of times. With a variable-speed control, you must develop the habit of winding the speed to zero before you hit the "on" button, and never stand in the firing line (90 degrees to the lathe axis, where a loose blank can be thrown) as you switch the lathe on.

The speed control gives you infinite variation between zero and that speed, so you can alter the speed with greater precision in the lower-speed range.

TOOL RESTS

Like the other components that make up a lathe, the tool-rest assembly needs to be heavily constructed. But because you move the rest frequently in order to have it as near the cut as possible, it needs to be easy to shift around. The easier it is to move and the more secure and solid it is when it's fixed, the better.

Typically two components make up the rest assembly: the banjo (base) and the T-rest. You

The tool rest should be adjustable so you can work on any part of the job no matter how the work is held.

should be able to lock the assembly in position on either side of a large bowl as shown in the photo above. To accomplish this, some lathes provide an additional short bed attached to the front of the headstock.

I like to move the whole rest assembly using one hand so that I can keep the tool I'm using in the other, saving time and maintaining work flow. The banjos with cam-action locks found on most of the better lathes work best, although I've found some to be a bit too heavy for me to move with ease. Try moving the assembly around using one hand when appraising a lathe. Avoid systems that require you to pick up a wrench or Allen key: They get lost in the shavings.

The best T-rests are cast iron, which absorbs vibration better than steel (see the

The best T-rests are cast iron (right), which absorbs vibration better than the steel rests to the left. T-rests should be set at an angle on the tool post and tapered. Curved rests reduce the leverage when hollowing and finishing inside deep bowls.

photo above). The most useful T-rests are set at an angle on the tool post and tapered in cross section. Curved rests allow you to support the tool closer to the cut when hollowing and finishing inside deep bowls.

The tool post supporting the rest should be at least 1 in. (25mm) in diameter on small lathes with a swing of less than 10 in. (250mm) or 1¼ in. (30mm) on larger machines. Make sure you can fix the rest at least ½ in. (13mm) above and below center height.

Choosing a Lathe

When I started out in 1970, the lathe I purchased promised everything I thought I could want. But within a few weeks, it proved woefully inadequate for almost every aspect of woodturning except small spindles between centers. I

replaced the drive shaft twice and broke several faceplates and rests. It was an expensive lesson, but its successor served me well for nearly 20 years before I replaced it with a lathe of slightly larger capacity and a much better tailstock.

Seductive promotional material for that first lathe featured a young lad turning a 4-ft. (1,200mm)-diameter table or bowl (or something) on a swivel headstock; size rendered the identity of the object of secondary interest. I had no idea then how challenging such large work is, but I found out a few years later when turning a 28-in. (710mm)-diameter bowl on a borrowed lathe well up to the task. I never felt the urge to make another bowl that size. Turning larger diameters with the work spinning so slowly is a totally different experience and not one I particularly enjoyed compared with working on a smaller scale at higher speeds, even though the result was satisfying.

For years I worked well within the 19-in. (480mm) maximum swing of my Harrison lathe. On the lathes I use now, I can swing 23½ in. (600mm), although I rarely do, partly because suitable chunks of wood that size are getting scarce, but mostly because few people can accommodate such large-scale work in their homes.

Your choice of lathe should be guided by a realistic assessment of the sort of bowls you're likely to make. Bear in mind that a 16-in. (405mm) bowl is huge and that a good-sized family salad bowl is 12 in. by 4 in. (305mm by 100mm). For most people, wood that size is difficult to come by and the task of turning it is mentally and physically exhausting—though there's satisfaction once the job is completed.

Few turners need a swing in excess of the 16 in. (405mm)
currently offered on most mid-sized lathes.

For those interested in working on a grander scale,
there are two options: monster lathes that are manufactured
with prices to match, or a lathe you build yourself.

My observation is that few turners need a swing in excess of the 16 in. (405mm) currently offered on most mid-sized lathes. A 23½-in. (600mm) swing or thereabouts should accommodate your wildest fantasies, as well as hollow vessels and deep vases. If the largest bowl you're likely to turn is for the family salad or fruit, a 12-in. (305mm) lathe should suffice. If you have only limited space, are on a limited budget, or are simply content to work on a smaller scale, there are a number of excellent small lathes that allow you to turn a reasonably sized bowl, as shown in the photo on p. 16.

You can also buy a lathe without a stand or motor—known as a bare lathe—or even just a headstock, then construct your own stand and rest support. If you opt for not having a tail center, this can be a comparatively inexpensive way to get well set up.

For those interested in working on a grander scale, there are two options: monster lathes that are manufactured with prices to match, or a lathe you build yourself. Superbly manufactured machines, such as the VB36 Master Bowlturner Lathe, are constructed to cope with very large, heavy, and off-balance chunks of wood. But for work of less than 20-in. (510mm) diameter I find them infuriatingly slow to operate. Adjusting the rest assembly of the VB36, with its cumbersome T-rest, is particularly tedious when working on a smaller scale.

Some manufacturers, such as Oneway and Vicmarc, offer an outboard thread adapter and reversing switch that enable right-handers to turn very large diameters outboard. This solution saves having two lathes, but it does require a lot of space all around the headstock.

If you want to work large on a limited budget, you should consider making your own lathe, using a spindle machined to accept the standard chucks and faceplates available through specialist woodturner's supply stores and catalogs. Err on the side of over-construction and weight, using the specifications of the larger manufactured lathes as a guideline. Adapting a heavy metalworking lathe is another option.

If you decide to build your own lathe, the good news is that for bowl turning you can generally manage without a tailstock because most work is firmly gripped by a chuck or on a faceplate. All you need is a drive shaft about 1¼ in. (30mm) in diameter set in substantial bearings about 10 in. (250mm) apart on a good base. The base can be a block of solid concrete (if your floor will take the weight) or heavy wood or steel beams. Over the years I've encountered many incredibly substantial bowl lathes built for very little cash outlay, although often requiring a great deal of labor and time. Many look pretty strange, but they do the job and have been used to produce thousands of wonderful bowls.

Equipment for Health and Safety

Concerns for health and safety begin with setting up your lathe and include ancillary equipment as well as procedures.

SETTING UP YOUR LATHE

You can have the best lathe in the world (can such a machine exist!), but if it's not properly set up, it won't be that enjoyable to use and you can end up with a sore back, tennis elbow, and the like.

It pays to set the center height so it's comfortable for you. You need to be able to see what you're doing without bending, so the best height for the lathe center is about 2 in. (50mm) above your elbow. If you are setting up a lathe to be used by a number of people, set it for the tallest and provide a platform for those shorter. Stacked sheets of 1-in. (25mm) MDF or chipboard are ideal, and defective or cover

I alternate between two lathes, so I keep my chucks and abrasives in a chest of drawers on wheels. The floor mat (old conveyor belting) makes standing on concrete all day less arduous. Shavings get caught on the rear bench and swept straight into a bag at the end.

sheets are often available very cheaply at builder's supply depots. You can use the same sheet materials to strengthen lightweight lathes and create benches around the workshop.

DUST EXTRACTION

Dust is a serious fire and health hazard, and if at all possible you should aim for the sort of dust- and shavings-free workshop that insurance agents dream we have. Obviously the long spirally shavings that make bowl turning so enjoyable will readily ignite, as will the fine sanding dust that settles beneath your grinder when hit by sparks as you sharpen your tools. The wire wool you might use when finishing should also be kept well clear of any sparks from the grinder.

Breathing fine dust can often lead to bronchial problems and allergies, and in a typical wood workshop there is more than wood dust to worry about. There are also the more insidious dusts from the grinding wheels, abrasives, and the resins that hold the abrasives together. These dusts are often fine enough to pass through most filtration systems, making the dust you can't see the real hazard. The fungus in spalted woods often likes dark, damp places to breed, and your lungs are just the ticket. I gave up turning spalted woods along with chemically treated lumber years ago when I found it affected my breathing.

All woodworking machines should have dust extraction, and the lathe is no exception. Unfortunately the lathe is one of the most difficult machines from which to collect. You won't catch the bulk of the heavier shavings, but you can get most of the dust if you have collection hoods both in front of and behind the headstock as shown in the photos at left and at left on the facing page. My new workshop is fitted with a 3-hp Delta system with a cyclone collector that removes air from the workspace. The air is much cleaner than previously and there is less dust settling overnight. Also I have a micro-

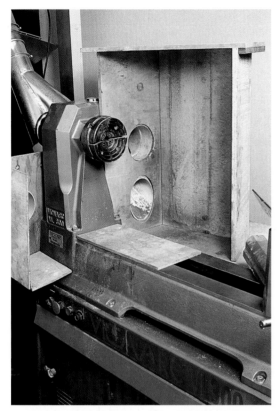

To gather up the dust when sanding a bowl, you need collecting points to the front and rear of the headstock. These collecting hoods are hinged so they can swing clear and not hinder the tools as cutting proceeds.

A large fan provides efficient dust extraction, but you don't want close neighbors.

filter air cleaner that removes most of the fine airborne particles that used to be visible only in shafts of sunlight. In winter the loss of warm air in a cold climate is a problem. I have in-slab floor heating and a workshop designed to collect the sun's heat, so I remain warm even on cold days when temperatures are barely above freezing. In the cold Northern Hemisphere, you'll need to recirculate the extracted air back into the workspace through a microfilter.

Of course, a steady breeze through open windows and doors removes dust, too, especially when aided by a big fan as shown in the photo at right above, but you need to be living in a suitable climate for that.

FACE SHIELDS

You should always wear a face shield when turning bowls because you never know when the wood might fly apart. Always remember that it's not a question of "if" but rather of "when," and then remember that you cannot be sure you'll be out of range when it happens.

Whenever I'm at the lathe I wear a helmet that combines an air-filtration system with an impact-resistant face shield that on several occasions has probably saved my life and at the very least prevented some spectacular scars and saved a number of teeth and an eye or two. There are a number of similar helmets on the market, mostly with the battery and filter on a waist pack connected to the helmet by a hose. When buying a helmet, look for a tilt-up visor, so if you need to speak to anyone or look at the work more closely, you can do so without removing the helmet.

CHUCK OPTIONS

The three primary options for mounting a bowl are using a screw chuck, a self-centering chuck, and a faceplate. The self-centering chucks and screw chucks are normally purchased as an option for the lathe, while faceplates are usually supplied as original equipment.

A screw chuck is the quickest and easiest way to grip a blank on the lathe.

Standard faceplates (on the table) and a drive (front) come standard with most lathes. You can adapt a faceplate to a wide drive (on the lathe). Drives need tail-center support.

A range of different jaws is available for most chucks. Changing jaws takes time, so having each set on its own body is a handy option for hobbyists and a necessity for professionals.

Fixings: Chucks, Faceplates, and Drives

Traditionally at least one faceplate is supplied with a new lathe, along with a small spur drive provided primarily for centerwork, although that can be useful for mounting small bowls between centers. Since being introduced in the mid 1980s, self-centering four-jaw chucks have become an essential element on any wood lathe used for more than just spindle turning.

There are quite a few self-centering four-jaw chucks commercially available, each with sets of interchangeable jaws designed for various aspects of turning. These chucks hold the work either by expanding into a recess or clamping around a foot or rim. By far the most useful for bowl turners are the step jaws, which can grip several different diameters without marking the wood and also expand into a recess slightly larger than the diameter of the jaws.

Avoid jaws that are heavily serrated; these might grip well, but they mark the wood, and getting rid of those marks always adds an extra step in the completion of a bowl. Plain dovetail jaws will grip just as well.

Information on the pros and cons of the various ways to fix wood or a partially completed bowl on the lathe in a given situation is covered near the beginning of each of chapters 4 through 8.

Tools

Having the right tools, set up so they are comfortable for you and effective for the task at hand, makes turning easier and therefore more enjoyable. Manufacturers offer a bewildering array of lathe tools, but you can get by with comparatively few. Here's my advice on acquiring a tool kit and some comments on handles.

GOUGES AND SCRAPERS

Bowls are turned using gouges and scrapers, and these come in a wide variety of shapes and sizes. Tools for all aspects of woodturning come as standard or long-and-strong, and, as their name implies, the latter are longer and stronger and altogether more robust than the standard tools. For bowl turning you generally need the heavier tools, especially when hollowing and the point of cut is well away from the rest.

Gouges are either deep-fluted or shallow. Deep-fluted gouges are made and marketed for bowl turning, while shallow gouges tend to be marketed as spindle gouges (for detailing in centerwork). Although it's possible to use just about any gouge for turning bowls, provided it is strong enough, wide centerwork roughing gouges—1 in. (25mm) and larger—should never be used for making bowls.

Broadly speaking, woodturning tools are made of either high-speed steel (HSS) or carbon steel. An HSS edge lasts about six times as long as a carbon-steel edge. It is designed to withstand high working temperatures, so careless grinding, which "blues" and ruins a carbon-steel

A variety of handles make tools easier to identify on the bench.

The top of this shear scraper is being polished on an old 100-grit sanding disc to create a better edge.

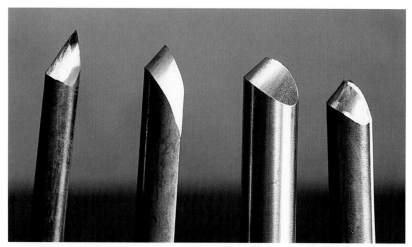

The four gouges I have in almost constant use are (from left) ⅜-in. (9mm) deep-fluted, ½-in. (13mm) deep-fluted, ½-in. (13mm) shallow, and ⅜-in. (9mm) shallow.

edge, has little effect on HSS. HSS is more expensive but definitely the way to go.

Most of the best tools continue to be manufactured in Sheffield, the English city long renowned for producing top-quality edge tools. The big names to look for are Henry Taylor, Ashley Isles, and Robert Sorby, and I favor these along with the American Glaser tools. Any HSS tool with Sheffield on it is usually worth con-

sideration, although the quality of finish varies, and this is reflected in the price. At the top end of the market, the tools are polished. Primarily this enables you to get a better cutting edge, but the tools also slide more easily along the tool rest and they feel better in the hand. The sharp corners and machining marks on less well-finished tools can be removed with coarse abrasives or a diamond hone. Machining marks on the upper surface of a blade can be polished out using fine abrasives or hones as shown in the top photo at left.

Avoid tools with an HSS tip laminated to a cheaper but stronger carbon-steel tool blade. The manufacturer's idea is to provide a less expensive tool using only a small amount of HSS. It's a nice idea that works quite well for square-ended scrapers in a nonproduction situation, but you soon grind away the HSS section then have to throw away the blade. Gouge inserts disappear even faster, and in addition the flute is rarely long enough for the popular long fingernail grind. In contrast, as solid HSS tools become shorter you can continue to use them on smaller bowls and on cuts close to the rest, eventually using up to 90 percent of the blade.

I have four gouges and five scrapers, as shown in the photos at left and on the facing page, in constant use and another half dozen of each that see a little action every few months. And there are a number that I don't use at all but looked pretty handy at the time I acquired them.

The ideal gouges for turning bowls range from ¼ in. (6mm) to ¾ in. (19mm). The popular ⅜-in. (9mm) and ½-in. (13mm) gouges are all you need for bowls up to 16 in. (405mm) in diameter and 4 in. (100mm) deep. Above that size, a longer and heavier ⅝-in. (16mm) or ¾-in. (19mm) gouge makes the job easier. If you intend to work only on a small scale, say, less than 6 in. (150mm) in diameter, ¼-in. (6mm) and ⅜-in. (9mm) gouges are all you need.

A basic scraper kit needs only one heavy 1¼-in. (32mm) by ⅜-in. (9mm) radius scraper for internal hollowing and a lighter-weight 1-in. (25mm) shear scraper for finishing a profile. After that, optional acquisitions include another large tool with a tighter radius, a spear-point scraper, and a skewed shear scraper.

HANDLES

Handles for bowl-turning tools need to be long to help you control the leverage and possibility of severe catches. Tools used for hollowing need heavier handles because cutting is often well over the rest. Traditionally handles have been made of wood and anywhere up to 2 ft. (61mm) long. However, my favorites are the extruded aluminum handles, loaded with lead shot to increase their weight, into which Glaser tools are fitted.

You could make your own (without the lead shot) by drilling a hole the same diameter as your gouge in the end of a length of a 1³⁄₁₆-in. (30mm) aluminum rod. The hole is best drilled by an engineering company set up for these tasks. Set the gouge in place with thin cyanoacrylate glue (Super Glue), but wrap a cloth around the blade to shield yourself from the cyanoacrylate. To remove a gouge glued into an aluminum handle, melt the glue by heating the contact area between the blade and handle with a gas torch and twist the two apart.

Also worth considering are the plastic-coated handles in which blades are fixed by grub screws. These are excellent for scrapers with a flat tang, which cannot be glued into a round hole.

Sharpening

Everyone knows that sharp tools are easier and much safer to use than blunt ones, so it's essential for turners to learn how to touch up an edge quickly on the grinding wheel. Sharp for bowl turning is an edge straight from a 60- or 80-grit grinding wheel complete with a small burr. By

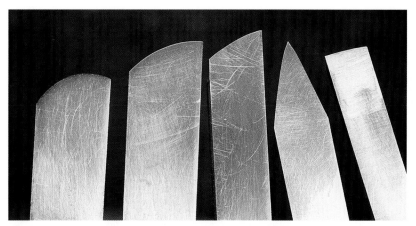

My essential scrapers are (from left) two 1¼-in. by ⅜-in. (32mm by 9mm) scrapers with slightly different radiuses, a 1-in. (25mm) shear scraper with a rounded left side, a 1-in. (25mm) spear-point, and a ¾-in. (19mm) square-end.

keeping the inside of a gouge flute or the top of a scraper polished or honed, you'll maintain a finer and more controlled burr.

GRINDERS

The small high-speed grinders universally available through hardware stores are commonly found in all types of workshops. They run fast at about 2,900 rpm to 3,600 rpm. Better but more expensive are those running much slower in the range of 1,400 rpm to 1,800 rpm. Both types of grinder typically come with carborundum wheels, which are fine for carbon steels but only adequate for today's HSS turning tools. These are better ground using the white friable aluminum oxide wheels formulated for that purpose. Friable means that they break down during use, constantly exposing new particles. Have one wheel that is 36 grit for reshaping and another 60 or 80 grit for finishing off and touching up an edge.

The larger the grinder the better. However, few of us can justify owning a large industrial grinder and instead settle for an 8-in. (200mm) model, then work on progressively smaller wheels as they wear away. Look for a rapid start-up. Some grinders take several seconds to build up speed, and if you are switching it on every few minutes, this can add up to several minutes a day standing around waiting for the grinder.

Grinding wheels, even friable wheels, glaze as particles of metal build up in the surface, severely reducing cutting efficiency and accelerating the heat buildup that blues the tools. Grinding wheels need to be dressed, and the

best tool for the job is a diamond amalgam dresser like those shown in the top photo at left. It will seem fearfully expensive but is a "must have" the moment you've seen one in action. I use it to shape as well as dress the wheel, and I prefer a slightly convex surface to grind on.

A water-cooled grinding wheel, like that shown in the bottom photo at left, produces a finer edge. Grinding does take a little longer and the grinders are more expensive, but you cannot burn the tool edge. Typically any rough grinding is best done quickly and efficiently on a high-speed wheel.

GRINDING THE BEVEL

The rule regarding bevel angles is that there is no rule, no single set of correct angles for woodturning tools. In general you can't go far wrong with bevels around 45 degrees on gouges and scrapers. The best shearing cut comes from an edge presented at about 45 degrees to the oncoming wood, but it is the differing combinations of edges and bevels that enable you to get a gouge working safely with the bevel rubbing the wood in different situations (these combinations are discussed in later chapters).

The bevel ideally should be a single, curved, concave facet that matches the grinding wheel. A plethora of grinding jigs are commercially available, enabling you to grind a perfect bevel every time but not necessarily a useful edge. The perfect edges look wonderful, but many are very aggressive in use and difficult to control. No jig I ever used enabled me to grind exactly what I wanted, and most are fiddly to use, so I recommend learning to grind freehand. The bevel might not look as pretty, but what does that matter if the tool cuts better? More important is the ability to grind an edge for specific jobs in specific situations.

Most of the problems encountered by novice woodturners on both lathe and high-speed grinder result from a bull-in-a-china-shop, when-in-doubt-use-force approach. At the lathe

Diamond-wheel dressers are the best tool for keeping your grinding wheels clean and sharp.

Water-cooled grinders never burn an edge but grinding does take a little longer. Rough-grind the angle on a high-speed wheel, then finish on the water-cooled wheel.

When grinding a tool, bring the bevel heel against the grinding wheel, then raise the handle until sparks come over the top of the edge.

this approach, combined with a blunt tool, leads to catches and a general lack of control. At the grinder it produces ragged edges of a colorful blue and straw hue.

Think of grinding as proceeding in four steps:

1. Place the tool on the rest, pitched well up and clear of the wheel.
2. Pin the tool to the rest between finger and thumb.
3. Pivot the tool forward by raising the tool handle so that you bring the bevel heel into contact with the wheel as shown in the two left photos above.
4. Continue to raise the tool handle (so the edge pivots into the wheel) until sparks come over the edge as shown in the two top right photos

When the upper surface of a tool has been polished, a telltale sign that you have a sharp tool is a slight discoloration along the edge, seen here to the right, which contrasts with the slight highlight on the edge to the left.

If a tool isn't cutting easily, look for flat spots on the edge like the triangular area near the nose of this shallow gouge.

on p. 35. High-speed steel produces only a few sparks, so another telltale sign that you have a sharp tool is a slight discoloration along the edge as shown in the bottom right photo on p. 35.

Go gently and steadily without pushing the tool hard against the wheel. Minimal contact will do the job, leaving the tool cool enough that, straight from the wheel, it can be held ¾ in. (20mm) back from the edge for five to 10 seconds. Let the wheel come to the tool, rather than forcing the tool into the wheel.

To grind a scraper, keep the tool on the rest and simply swing the handle back and forth, as shown in the photo below. Gouges require a more complex movement, depending on the shape of the grind.

If a tool isn't cutting, look for flat areas or micro-bevels that catch the light as shown in the top photo at left. A common error when

To reshape an edge, grind both wings at the same time until the edge of the flute is a smooth curve.

To grind a scraper, keep the tool flat on the rest and swing the handle through an arc.

grinding gouges is to remove too much metal from the sides as you roll the tool over, creating an undulating edge rather than the full convex shape you need. To correct this or to create a fingernail-ground edge on a new gouge, hold the tool on its side, with the flute toward the grinder and the length of the tool almost parallel to the edge of the grinding wheel, so that you grind both wings of the edge at the same time as shown in the center photo at left on the facing page. Then swing the handle around so you round over the wings as shown in the bottom photo at left on the facing page. The idea is to obtain a smooth curve to the edge of the flute. Then when you grind away all the flat sections, you should have a perfect fingernail-ground edge.

When you need to adjust the bevel angle, have the tool on its side so you can look down and see the angle develop while you're grinding (see the photo at right). Then complete

grinding with the gouge in the usual position, rolling the tool and swinging the handle around and easing the edge slightly up the wheel to grind the side as shown in the bottom photos. If the side bevel needs to be longer than on the

Set a new bevel angle with the tool on its side so you can see what you're doing.

To grind the side of a gouge, swing the handle around and ease the edge up the wheel.

Ease the gouge up the wheel to grind the side.

A typical bevel ground on a small-diameter high-speed wheel.

nose of the tool, ease the tool up the wheel rather than swinging the handle around as shown in the photos above.

The center photo at left shows the sort of bevel you can expect using a small-diameter high-speed grinder. Note that the nose protrudes very slightly from the wings and that the edge is convex: A straightedge held against it will contact only one point at a time.

Saws

Sawing logs yourself and cutting your own blanks and discs gives you maximum control over your raw material and the opportunity to maximize the return from each board or log. You can use all the offcuts for smaller bowls, other turning projects, or burning. Fortunately a decent small bandsaw that can handle small logs up to 10 in. (250mm) in diameter won't cost the earth. If you have access to logs, a good small chainsaw can pay for itself in no time.

BANDSAWS

A good bandsaw is an essential tool for any bowl turner. Its major attributes are the ability to cut

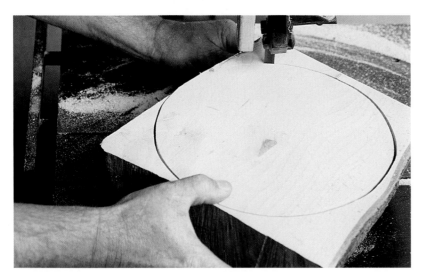

The ability to cut circles makes a bandsaw an essential tool for any bowl turner.

Although marketed as disposable, small band-saw blades can be reground on a high-speed grinder in a few minutes by lightly touching the top of each tooth.

circles and a narrow blade that minimizes waste when converting small logs.

The capacity of a bandsaw is defined by its throat and its depth of cut. The throat is the distance between the blade and the pillar supporting the upper wheel. The depth of cut is the maximum thickness you can cut.

The most important feature of any bandsaw used to convert small logs to bowl blanks is the depth of cut. The capacity on many small saws is only 6 in. (150mm), which is more than enough to cut discs from thick boards. For many small bandsaws, a riser kit enables you to increase the depth of cut to 12 in. (305mm). My Startrite, with a sharp blade and the blade guard removed, will cut 11½ in. (290mm).

BANDSAW SAFETY

When using a bandsaw, bear in mind the following important safety points.

1 Never adjust the guides while the saw is running.

2 Never open the doors or remove any guards while the saw is running.

3 Position the upper guides as close to the wood as possible.

4 Make sure the blade is not exposed above the upper guides.

5 Never leave the saw running unattended.

6 Make sure that the wood is supported below the blade; never saw overhangs.

7 Keep your hands well to the side or behind the blade or use a push stick.

8 Never force wood into the blade. If it's not cutting fast enough, the blade is dull, the wood is hard, or you're in too much of a hurry.

9 Dull blades are dangerous. They encourage you to push the wood so hard that the blade bends back. At the end of the cut, the blade springs forward; having your finger there to meet it is a common accident. Use sharp blades, and see rule number 7.

CHAINSAW SAFETY

Chainsaws are notoriously dangerous and noisy. They fire chips into your eyes and, if handled carelessly, can kick back and inflict horrendous injuries in a fraction of a second. Consequently, you should heed the following safety points.

1. Make sure your saw is fitted with an automatic chain brake.

2. Always wear ear and eye protection. Better still, wear a chainsaw helmet with ear guards and a face shield.

3. Don't reach in with your hand to reposition a blank while the chain is still running. Keep both hands on the saw while it's running.

4. Don't use your foot to stabilize any blank you are cutting.

5. Don't lean over a running saw, even if it's just idling.

6. Don't leave a chainsaw running unattended.

7. Don't cut while anyone else is within arm's length of your saw.

My bandsaw has a 13¾-in. (350mm) throat, which limits me to cutting only one blank larger than that out of a single board or slab. It's been a minor inconvenience over the years. A larger saw would be nice, but I never could justify the cost since I can't easily lift onto the saw most of the wood I'd want to cut. Chunks in excess of 66 lb. (30kg) are easier to cut on the ground using a chainsaw.

Bandsaw blades are defined by the width of the blade and the number of teeth per inch (tpi). As a basic rule, the thicker the wood you're cutting, the fewer the teeth. Most of the time I use a ¾-in. (19mm) blade with 3 or 4 tpi. This is ideal for breaking down large blocks and circles above 11 in. (280mm). It doesn't like going around corners much tighter but will if the blade is new. For diameters of 5 in. to 11 in. (125mm to 280mm), I use a ½-in. (13mm), 4-tpi blade and for even smaller blanks, I have ⅜-in. (9mm) and ¼-in. (6mm) blades.

Small bandsaw blades are normally marketed as disposable, however I've always reground them on a fine wheel as shown in the photo on p. 39. Typically I can regrind a blade up to 10 times before it breaks from metal fatigue. Each sharpening reduces a blade's ability to cut curves, but it cuts more aggressively.

Bandsaws are the subject of whole books and it's worth investing in a volume like Lonnie Bird's *The Bandsaw Book* (The Taunton Press, 1999) for more detailed information, especially if you want your saw to cut more than just bowl blanks.

CHAINSAWS

If you are working with logs more than 8 in. (200mm) in diameter, an electric or gasoline-powered chainsaw will make life a lot easier. Within range of electricity, an electric chainsaw is preferable; they are quieter, more reliable, and, because there are no fumes, usable indoors.

As a bowl turner, you will definitely need a collection of measuring tools including calipers, dividers, and rulers. Other tools I use frequently when rough-turning include a pipe wrench and small crowbar. There's also cyanoacrylate adhesive (Super Glue) for filling holes and splits.

I have a small electric saw with a 12-in. (305mm) bar and a bottom-of-the-professional-range gasoline-powered Husqvarna with a 20-in. (510mm) bar. By cutting in from either side or end of a log, you can cut a chunk of wood twice the length of the bar. I've never felt the need for a longer bar.

If you've never used a chainsaw, take a course that teaches you how to use one safely. Read the manual and learn how to maintain the saw and bar and keep the chain sharp.

Wooden wedges (which cannot damage the saw chain) and a splitting maul are often useful when chainsawing, as is an axe (wear steel-capped boots). Use a stiff, wire brush to clean away dirt and grit that might damage the chain. I wear heavy gloves against splinters and the venomous fauna that are never too far away in Australia.

Ancillary Tools

As a bowl turner, you will need measuring tools for laying out chuck diameters and measuring internal depths so you don't go through the bottom or side of your bowls and ruin everything. Dividers are also used for marking circles on boards to be cut into discs, so if you have only one pair, make sure they can scribe a reasonably large circle. Double-ended calipers are the best tools for checking wall thickness, and you'll need two rulers to measure internal depths accurately. You'll see most of the tools that are shown in the photo above in action in later chapters.

3 WOOD AND BOWL BLANKS

When I began turning bowls, the slightest defect, hole, or bark intrusion rendered the bowl a second, fit only to be sold cheaply. I gave many to friends who continue to use them 25 to 30 years later. The bowls have worn well and their so-called defects have long since vanished into the patina that comes with daily use. Fortunately in these days of greater ecological awareness, the use of wood with the odd borer hole is acceptable, even laudable, and bowls featuring bark intrusions or other irregularities are now considered attractive. Our change in attitude as to what is acceptable has mostly been for the good, for we now use wood that formerly would have gone straight to the wood heap for burning. Very spectacular bowls have emerged from many seemingly unpromising chunks of wood.

In 30 years I've made thousands of bowls, and because I never cared for the laminated look, each is turned from solid timber. The wood I use has come from a variety of sources. Much I have collected myself, but I've purchased the bulk of it from specialist dealers. Obtaining good raw material is essential, so this chapter suggests where you might find your raw logs or

cut blanks, what to look for, and the points you need to assess so you don't haul home stuff you can't or might not want to use. Finally there is information on cutting. But before getting to all that, let's consider how the properties of wood and what you want to do with it affect what you should buy and how you should store it.

Wood

Timbers are classified as hardwoods or softwoods. Hardwoods include most of the well-known fine woodworking timbers that come from broadleaf trees such as oak, ash, cherry, and maple. Softwoods encompass the more open-grained coniferous pines and cedars, which are not necessarily soft. However, the open end grain of most softwoods is very difficult to cut cleanly, so it is generally avoided for facework such as bowls where the end grain has to be cut cleanly twice on any profile and twice more on the inside. Besides that, bowls made from resinous softwoods do not make particularly good containers for foods.

The grain of any wood runs the length of the tree, which structurally is little more than a bundle of long fibers stuck together in rings of

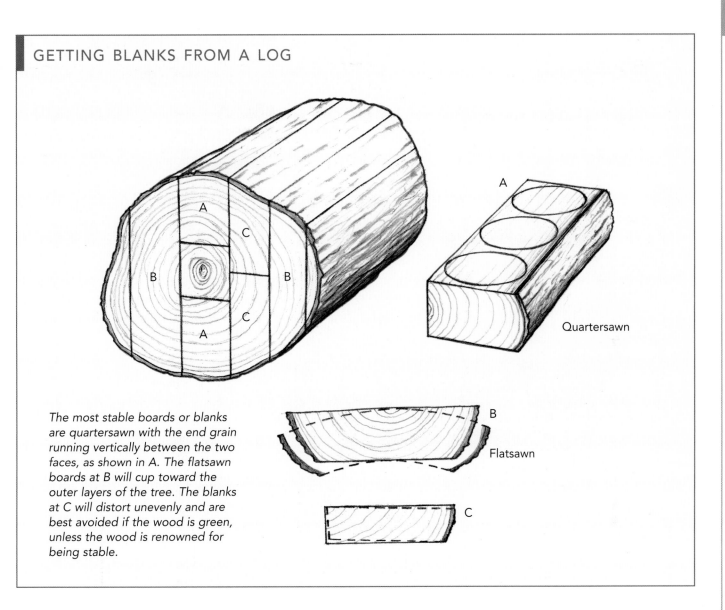

GETTING BLANKS FROM A LOG

A

C

B

B

C

A

A

Quartersawn

B

Flatsawn

C

The most stable boards or blanks are quartersawn with the end grain running vertically between the two faces, as shown in A. The flatsawn boards at B will cup toward the outer layers of the tree. The blanks at C will distort unevenly and are best avoided if the wood is green, unless the wood is renowned for being stable.

annual growth wrapped in bark. These fibers give timber great longitudinal strength (which is why lengths are used for tool handles), but their connection across the grain is weak, and they are easily separated along their length (axes effortlessly split for logs for firewood). For this reason, bowls should have the grain aligned parallel to the faces of the blank as shown in the illustration above.

Grain orientation in a bowl affects its strength and usability. If a bowl form is aligned

in a blank with its top and bottom facing the end grain so the grain runs vertically in the blank, the base will be very fragile. In the photo at right on p. 44, you can see the fragility of end grain: A heavy knock could easily punch a hole on such a thin section of short grain if it were located in the base of a bowl, and a sharp blow to the side could likewise split it along its length. Consequently, if you drop an end-grain bowl (as this grain orientation is called), it will probably break. A cross-grain bowl (where the

Huon Pine Bowl

It is rare to be able to include the pith of a log in a bowl, for few timbers are as stable as this. With most woods I would expect that eventually the pith will split or distort.

| MATERIAL: | Huon pine |
| SIZE: | 6 in. by 3 ⅜ in. (150mm by 85mm) |

The best place to obtain woodturning stock is from one of the many specialist dealers catering to the demands of fine woodworkers or woodturners.

Always cut a thin slice from the end of a board or log and bend it to check that there are no hidden splits. Cracks like these can often remain unrevealed until the latter stages of sanding or finishing.

grain runs parallel to the base and rim) will split only if dropped directly on the end-grain portion of the wood.

As wood dries, it shrinks *across* the grain (in diameter or in width) but hardly at all *along* the grain (in length). Cross-grain bowls turned from green wood will therefore dry into an oval shape.

The outer layers of logs shrink more than those nearer the center, so splits occur from the outside in. If you are unable to convert a log before it starts cracking, split it down the center on the line of any radial defect, and that should limit further splitting from the outer layers.

The ends of boards and logs dry faster than the interior and will split unless sealed to slow drying to the same rate throughout.

Boards will distort as they dry out, as shown in the illustration on p. 43, but they won't necessarily crack, especially if the grain is of fairly even density. The most stable boards or blanks are quartersawn, the growth rings running perpendicular to the two faces (see the photo on the facing page). Quartersawn boards will shrink more in thickness than in width and will not cup. Flatsawn boards will shrink more in width than in thickness, and the face toward the outer layers of the tree will shrink more than the face toward the center, causing the board to cup toward the outer layers. The blanks with some of each grain will distort erratically and are best avoided if the wood is green, unless the species is renowned for being stable. If the pith is off-center, warping will be uneven.

Unfortunately we bowl turners tend to be interested in wood with swirling grain and dramatic figure that rarely dries in large sections without splitting. To overcome this problem, it is best to work the wood before it splits, turning it green into thick rough bowls that warp as they dry but rarely split—assuming you start with sound material.

Hundreds of books have been written describing the properties and workability of just about every wood. Your local library should be able to provide access to at least some of them. And, of course, there's the Internet. But there's nothing like sifting through real books. I've collected most of my wood books browsing around bookstalls and flea markets dealing in secondhand volumes, and I always check out bookstores I come across as well. Look also for the regular articles on woods in woodworking periodicals.

FINDING WOOD

The world's forests are being seriously depleted so that more affluent sections of the world's community can read fatter newspapers, eat cheaper hamburgers, and use disposable tissues rather than washable cloth. But there's still plenty of wood we woodturners can use with a clear conscience. While a few professional turners will need to search out whole trees for their runs of bowls, studio turners and hobbyists can make good use of just about any odd chunk or short length typically discarded by other woodworkers.

Flatsawn blanks (left) are less stable than quartersawn blanks (right). The flatsawn will yield more interesting patterns inside the bowl.

In addition, since the late 1970s much wood previously considered defective and barely fit for a fireplace is now used for what are termed artistic bowls—that is, bowls with holes, irregularities, or other features formerly regarded as defects but now used for decorative effect.

Wood is commercially available from sawmills, lumberyards, and some specialty woodturning supply stores. The nearer to the tree you are (metaphorically speaking), the larger the chunks or boards available, the lower the price, and the more you have to buy at one time. In rural areas, you might be lucky enough to be near a mill that saws fresh logs, but most mills don't welcome small-time buyers interested only in a few odd bits of wood. Stores will deal mostly in kiln-seasoned lumber, although increasingly some carry turning blanks along with turning tools.

The best place to obtain woodturning stock is from one of the many specialist dealers cater-

There are so many woods known to work easily that it seems a foolish waste of time to seek out the tough and difficult stuff.

Specialist stores, like this one in Calgary, stock a wide range of seasoned boards and thick squares suitable for turning.

ing to the demands of fine woodworkers or woodturners in particular. These companies can sell you a wide variety of wood in almost any condition, from logs to short boards, from slabs to cylindrical blanks, as shown in the photo above. Many advertise widely in specialist wood and woodturning magazines and often have Web sites with up-to-date stock lists. If you don't have a bandsaw, some dealers can sell you blanks already cut round and prepared for mounting on the lathe.

For those with saws, where there are trees there will be tree surgeons, municipal and pub-lic utility crews, and neighbors pruning and felling trees and sizeable woody shrubs in streets, gardens, and parks. Storms yield wonderful windfalls, literally. All you have to do is keep your eyes open and be prepared to shove the odd log in the back of your vehicle (a powerful argument for having a small truck or van so you can take advantage of any opportunity). Collect branches in sections as long as you can manage. If you need to saw a log in half, cut it lengthways along the pith and divide it, as necessary, in multiples of the log's diameter (more of this in the next section). Even a 6-in.

(150mm) log can yield 5-in. (125mm) bowls, so a lot of tree thinnings are worth considering.

I'm equipped to collect my own lumber with two chainsaws, a van, and a small trailer. When necessary, I can haul about 1½ tons at one time. When I locate a tree, I cut it into manageable pieces, even if there is equipment or manpower to load whole logs onto my trailer. I want to be able to move it off my trailer as well as on, so I slab or split larger pieces to a size I can handle myself. For the trip home, I cover the end grain with plastic or a tarpaulin to limit the airflow that dries and splits a freshly sawn surface.

If you are unable to turn green wood immediately, store it out of direct sunlight with the ends sealed to retard splitting. Wax emulsions are commercially available, but cling-wrap is a cleaner alternative. Sealing the end grain is no guarantee against splitting, but it will delay the inevitable. Woods that like to split will do so eventually unless rough-turned, in which condition they'll typically warp.

Sealing end grain, or even the whole blank, delays the inevitable. Woods that are prone to splitting, like the Tasmanian myrtle (right), will do so after a few months seasoning, despite being sealed. Sealing more stable woods like the she-oak and jarrah (left) usually prevents any degradation of the end grain.

WHAT TO LOOK FOR

Whenever I go hunting for or buying wood, be it logs, boards, or blanks, I'm looking for the same things. I'm not interested in ridiculously expensive woods, no matter how good the grain or the color, which I know will fade soon enough. Since I earn my living selling bowls, I want a wood that is easy to work. I've enjoyed turning hundreds of different species over the years and learned a lot, but for production and teaching I prefer to avoid anything famous for being very hard or particularly difficult to work.

There are so many woods known to work easily, smell nice, and take the fine detail of beads and coves that it seems a foolish waste of time to seek out the tough and difficult stuff. As a general rule, you cannot go far wrong with any species used by the furniture trades, which demand stable and easy-to-work wood. Cherry, ash, mahogany, teak, maple, and walnut are all dependable although often a bit bland. You can usually find these woods in specialist wood-working stores and from hardwood dealers. Most likely the boards will have been kiln-dried and, if devoid of splits, can be purchased with confidence. All the grain-alignment decisions will have been made for you at the sawmill, so all you have to do is cut your discs and get turning.

As a professional, I need also to work within market demands, which for me currently are for heavier bowls in red woods, preferably with plenty of dramatic figure and defects for character. There was a time when plainer wood was easier to sell, but for the moment I buy a lot of jarrah and redgum burl for big chunky forms, rather than collecting the ash or elm I'd prefer to be turning into finer bowls. I like to get my wood unseasoned before it starts to deteriorate, and I look for logs and boards without splits and knots, or burls with uniform grain that will dry evenly. Ideally trees should be harvested in late autumn and into winter when the sap is at

The sanded section (lower right) gives a better idea of the flashy grain that can be difficult to discern on the sawn surface. The hairy surface on the rear blank indicates that the grain will be difficult to cut cleanly.

its lowest, then boards and roughed bowls can start to season before the stressful heat of summer.

You can get some idea of what you're likely to find inside a log or board in terms of grain patterns, color, and working difficulties by looking carefully at the outside and ends. The surface on sawn lumber soon darkens, so to find out what the color is, scrape the surface and moisten it with water (spit is most common) or oil to bring out the color, as shown in the photo at left. If you don't carry a knife or scraper, many retailers will provide you with one, or they might have finished samples on view. Scraping a face clean gives you a view only of the surface. For a more thorough picture, examine the end grain for variations in color and splits, especially radial splits that go to the pith and run along most of the length of a log. Check the density of the annual growth rings. If the softer wood between the growth rings is smooth and free of torn grain, there's a good

The grain patterns and fiddleback figure in this 20-in. by 4½-in. (510mm by 115mm) camphor laurel are typical of wood cut from a crotch.

chance the wood will work well or at least cut cleanly. But it might be hard.

The blanks shown in the photo on p. 47 are about three years old and typical of what you might find in a store. To the left, there are no problems with splits, and the woods are well known for being stable. The split in the upper of the two myrtle blanks to the right turned away, and the ridged top corners indicate a heavy quilt figure. The photo on p. 51 shows how that grain looks when finished. The large 12-in. by 4-in. (305mm by 100mm) blank below has good color variations but has split badly. However, by cutting along the main splits, I salvaged a number of smaller bowls 4 in. (100mm) in diameter as well as blanks for other turning projects.

Dramatic grain like the highly prized quilted or fiddleback figure seen in the camphor laurel bowl in the bottom photo on the facing page can often be discerned on the outside of a tree or log as corrugations like those seen in the photos at right. Such flashy grain usually comes from stressed sections of the tree, typically around a branch or crotch. Small branches on large trees create knots that can be attractive and have interesting grain associated with them. But wood in these areas is stressed and therefore more likely to split than plain straight-grained wood. In the top photo at right, note that the small cracks in the area of the cutoff branch proved to be of little consequence nearer the trunk, with only a slight split from the pith evident.

Assessing trees and logs is always something of a lottery because you never know exactly what might be inside. Among the most obvious external signs of interesting grain are burls, which can be either single chunks, as shown in the top left photo on p. 50, or sometimes a whole trunk, as shown in the top right photo on p. 50. However, if the surface of a burl is absolutely smooth, chances are that the inside

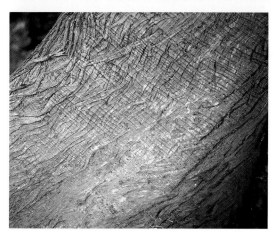

Fiddleback grain shows up as corrugations on the bark.

will be pretty bland with little or no grain or color variation.

The strong lines on end grain such as those seen on the casuarina board (bottom left) in the photo on p. 47, are rays. Any surface cut parallel to those lines will have a wide, ribbonlike pattern, so at least some parts of your bowl will have dramatic grain.

Damage high up a tree, typically where a broken limb leaves a hole where water can penetrate the trunk, can mean that the center will be stained as it begins to rot. A lot of interesting wood can be had before the rot sets in, although

Burls often yield dramatic grain.

This knobby eucalyptus trunk would almost certainly yield interesting grain patterns, but you can never be sure until the tree is on the ground and sliced.

The rotten and borer-ridden sapwood on the lower blank can be turned away, whereas the white flecking of incipient rot in the upper blank marks it for a fireplace despite the tight ripple grain.

having died, it will always look somewhat flat and lackluster. The best wood comes from living trees that are felled or otherwise killed suddenly. I have always found elm killed by Dutch elm disease to be excellent bowl-turning wood.

Dead and dying trees are attacked by various bugs, worms, and beetles, and you should look for their holes in the sap and outer layers of the tree. In the photo at left, borers have been through the white sappy area and into the heartwood, back-filling their holes as they go, which makes them difficult to see. Back-filled holes can be solidified with thin cyanoacrylate adhesive (see also p. 111 and p. 178). The white flecks in the tilted blank are rot and worth cutting out despite the rippled figure. Although such areas can be solidified, they never seem to enhance a finished surface.

You can encourage fungal attack on wood to induce dramatic spalting patterns by wrapping freshly cut wood in plastic for a few weeks. Be aware, however, that working spalted wood might be very bad for your lungs, which provide a nice warm, dark place for fungal spores to breed. I avoid spalted woods.

Converting Logs, Boards, and Burls into Blanks

In a perfect world, wood would be inert, never twisting or splitting as it seasons. A few hardwoods such as mahogany, maple, cherry, and jarrah are remarkably stable, but if you are dealing with wood that hasn't been kiln-dried, it's best to assume that it will split, warp, and twist before stabilizing. On p. 143, you'll see how warping can be used to good decorative effect.

Before you start cutting a log or board into blanks, you need to have an idea of how dry or wet it is. If you know when logs were harvested, you get some idea of their condition. Trees should be felled in late autumn and winter when they contain the least moisture. If lumber or a turning square hasn't been kiln-dried, ask how long it's been in the store or when it was cut. The longer it's been around the better. Many turning blanks originating in Australia such as jarrah and myrtle will have the month and year cut noted on them or the original weight in kilos. If this is almost double the actual weight of the blank, you'll know the wood is seasoned.

Several types of moisture meters are available through specialist woodturning suppliers, although only professionals can likely justify the expense. On the other hand, you get a fairly good idea when you cut into a chunk of wood how dry it is. Green wood drips moisture, and sawdust will be sticky and damp. Dry wood

Tasmanian Myrtle Bowl

Such high-quilted figure comes from a particularly stressed area of a tree, in this instance from the buttress of a Tasmanian myrtle tree growing on a steep slope. Such highly figured timber is frustratingly difficult to cut cleanly and sand, but the labor is worth the effort.

| MATERIAL: | Tasmanian myrtle |
| SIZE: | 11¾ in. (300mm) diameter |

Bowls roughed from evenly grained wood should warp symmetrically.

sawdust is powdery and stays airborne for some time. The cut surfaces of partially dry boards typically look like liquid spilt on dry cloth—obviously drier around a darker and damper center.

When converting freshly felled logs, burls, or boards straight from a sawyer, you'll need to take more care over the alignment of the grain than when cutting discs from partly seasoned lumber. Green wood will warp far more than dry, so the greener the timber, the more important it is to have the grain aligned within a blank symmetrically so the roughed bowl will warp evenly. Remember that quartersawn wood will shrink but not cup and that flatsawn blanks will cup toward the larger growth rings and away from the center of the tree. If the grain is evenly balanced on either side of the pith, you will get an even warp and an oval bowl as shown in the photo above. If the pith is off-center and the tighter growth rings associated with the center of a tree are to one side of the blank, your roughed bowl will warp into a D-shape, which will be difficult to rechuck, let alone retrieve a bowl from. Plain wood with

burly grain in one area will distort unevenly, as it also will around a knot or an area of high figure.

CUTTING LOGS

The size of bowls you intend to make and how soon you'll turn the blanks affect how you approach breaking down a log. When I get hold of a log, I like to cut it up and rough-turn it immediately before it even thinks of splitting. If the log is near a lathe, I cut only a few blanks at a time, rough-turning those before doing another batch. Even better was the time I was in Tasmania buying wood: I marked out blanks that my timber-getter bandsawed while I roughed bowls. We got through nearly a ton of wood that day. Green wood turns very easily, so any reasonably competent turner will have no problem converting a ton of logs to roughed bowls in a few days.

My approach to breaking down a log into bowl blanks is the same regardless of the size of the log. The scale of the operation and the saws you have available dictate precisely how you go about it. For larger logs you need a chainsaw, although if the timber is straight-grained and

SAWING WOOD SAFELY

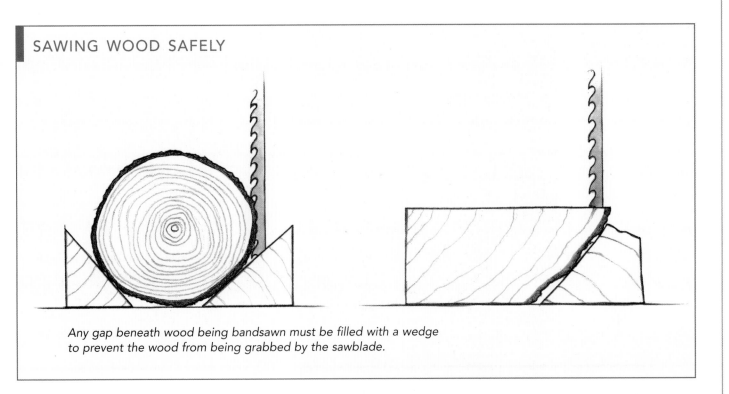

Any gap beneath wood being bandsawn must be filled with a wedge to prevent the wood from being grabbed by the sawblade.

you're into traditional techniques, splitting with wedges is an option. The face of a wedged slab is rarely smooth, but it might make for an interesting texture on a bowl rim.

Logs less than 12 in. (300mm) in diameter can be sawn entirely on a small bandsaw, although you might find docking lengths from a long log easier using a chainsaw or handsaw. For safety, round logs should be wedged to keep them from rolling into the saw as shown in the photo at right. There should never be space between the point where the sawblade enters the wood and the saw table; otherwise the downward pressure of the blade can bind the blade or snap the overhanging wood onto the table (see the illustration above). Consequently, any portion of a blank with space beneath it must be supported. When dealing with short sections of a log, always put them through the saw on an end cut square to the bark, as shown in the top left photo on p. 54.

Round logs must be wedged to prevent them from rolling into the saw.

When the whole width of the leg is usable, cut the leg on end to create flat faces.

Alternatively, put the log on its flat side in order to cut the slab, taking care not to have the blade enter an unsupported section of the log.

Split ends should be docked back to more solid wood. Here there is still a way to go.

I begin by docking short sections from the end until most of the splits are gone. Then I cut lengths equal to the diameter of the log, and cut these into slabs from which I cut round blanks. I square up all good-sized offcuts and flitches and put them aside for air-drying, later to be turned into boxes, small bowls, and small production items. Sales of objects made from the offcuts should more than pay for the wood.

When cutting back to solid wood on the end of a log (or board), it's easy to miss the finer splits. No matter how dry the wood, it pays to cut a thin slice off the end grain, then bend it slightly. This habit can save you a lot of grief later because many of the finest splits show up only in the latter stages of finishing. In

When the length of the log is less than the width, mark the length on the end grain to establish the overall dimensions of the blank (above). Cut the log on end, first the width of the blank, then the faces (left).

the bottom photo on p. 54, the last of the three slices broke easily, revealing there's still a way to go.

Initial cuts down a log should be along the line of the major split and through the pith to get a defect-free face. Subsequent cuts, parallel to the first cut, create the slabs from which you cut the discs. Where the full width of the log can be used, the short length is cut on end, with a second slice taken to obtain a broader face on what will be the top of the blank of an enclosed form. You can see a split at the base of a branch sawn off in the first cut, and any remaining crack will go when the bowl is hollowed. The fiddleback figure should show up around the rim and sides of the bowl.

If an end-grain slice reveals splits that cannot be seen on the log, align a section of the slice in its original position and trace around the edge to mark the splits on the log.

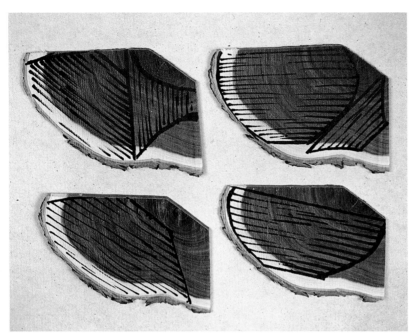

Here are four ways you might align bowls within a typical flitch. To the left, the bowls will have bark rims; to the right, each will have a single splash of the white sapwood up the side.

When cutting a board into blanks, it's often possible to gain a few small bowls from the offcuts between the main bowls. The lines on the large blanks highlight the defects so that end-grain splits will be easier to locate as the profile is turned.

When the length of the log is less than its width as shown in the top right photo on p. 55, mark the length on the end grain to establish the dimensions of the blank and cut the log on end as shown in the photo at left on p. 55. Alternatively, set the log on the flat face created by the first cut on the saw table (see the top right photo on p. 54) and cut a slab from which you can cut a disc. If you use dividers or a compass to scribe the circle, there will be a mark left by the point at center, which will be easy to locate later when you mount the blank on the lathe.

CUTTING BURLS AND ODD-SHAPED CHUNKS

When dealing with odd-shaped blanks, the secret to working safely is to cut a flat face, which provides a firm base for subsequent cuts. Thus to get a natural-edge bowl from a typical small burl, I scribe a circle using dividers as shown in the top photo at right on the facing page, then cut a series of facets up to the circle, always keeping a flat surface against the saw table (see the center and bottom photos at right on the facing page). It may look untidy, but provided there's a base reasonably parallel to the top into which the tail center can go, there should be few problems mounting the blank (see the top photos on p. 70). And keep your eye out for offcuts large enough to turn into small bowls.

BOWLS FROM BOARDS

Sawmills slice large logs lengthwise into boards, and if the wood is even-grained and defect-free, it stands a good chance of drying without splitting. Bowl turners should use short boards that yield only two or three bowls at most. I believe that, in our world of dwindling resources, turners should leave long boards that can be used for

This 7-in. (180mm)-diameter log yielded a number of small, natural-edged bowls.

If you're halfway through cutting a blank that suddenly looks too tall, flip the blank on the remaining flat face and cut it as required. You might consider cutting a rounded blank in a similar way, using wedges to stabilize the blank, but it's difficult to hold the wedges and blank securely and is not recommended.

When marking out and cutting multifaceted blocks like this burl offcut, ensure that you always have a flat facet on the saw table supporting the cut.

Claret Ash Bowls

These little bowls are made from the sort of small offcuts usually discarded. I reckon that the sales of bowls made from such waste will pay for the blank. Galleries like them for cash flow.

MATERIAL: Claret ash

SIZES: 4 in. (100mm) maximum diameter

Bowl turners should be using short boards that yield only two or three bowls at most.

cabinetmaking to cabinetmakers, who in turn can leave all their offcuts for turners. A cabinet-maker's waste bin is usually full of dry offcuts suitable for turning, and although this potential bowl material is rarely more than 2 in. (50mm) thick, that's ideal for many projects.

Seasoning

It has been said that wood is at its best and strongest after several hundred years, and my limited experience in turning timber from ancient beams rescued from English barns and churches confirms this. The shavings don't pour off the gouge as they do from green wood full of sap, but the dry wood cuts very cleanly and there are few problems even on normally difficult end grain.

Sadly, few of us get to work wood of this quality, but if you have prime timber devoid of rot and can keep boring insects at bay, the longer you can let your wood air-dry the better. If you have the space, it pays to lay down stocks of sawn lumber for the years ahead. I always have some thicker stock laid down for unusual orders when time doesn't allow for seasoning. This stock is ideal for projects such as the set of small bowls shown in the photo on the facing page.

The old rule of thumb for air-drying hard-woods of medium density is one year per inch of thickness, plus one year. This means a 2-in. (50mm) board will take three years to dry, and typical salad bowl material will take anywhere from five to seven years to air-dry in solid chunks.

Kiln-drying is an economically viable option for boards up to 3 in. (75mm) thick. For any greater thickness, kiln-drying is inefficient and expensive. Kiln-dried wood is not very pleasant to work, being very dusty and occasionally chemically treated to boot. The working qualities of air-dried timber are far superior, so I avoid kiln-dried wood whenever possible.

Like most bowl turners, I find the time and space required for air-drying to be a problem. You get from 60 to 70 salad bowls to your ton, so stocks of solid timber demand a lot of space for years to come. And even after all the seasoning, there's no guarantee that the wood will remain stable; when you remove the center of a blank to create a bowl, the altered stresses often cause the form to warp.

A bowl turner can reduce the whole seasoning process to a few months by rough-turning bowls when the wood is green, at the same time avoiding the tedious task of always working dry wood. I find that 6-in. to 8-in. (15mm to 20mm) bowls roughed in April (Australian autumn) are ready for finishing by November the same year (just in time for the Christmas market). Bowls that are 12 in. to 14 in. (305mm to 355mm) in diameter are not really stable for at least a year, and two years is better, unless the wood is almost inert.

Rough-Turning

The principle of rough-turning is to partly turn the bowl when the wood is easiest to work, then set it aside to dry. When it is dry, you remount it for completion. The wall thickness of a rough-turned bowl should be about one-tenth the diameter of the bowl. Thus a 4-in. (100mm)-high bowl with a wall thickness of 1 in. (25mm) will dry in a quarter of the time of the solid board from which it was cut. Whenever possible, I rough-turn bowls and season the wood in that form because it will stabilize in a few months rather than years. The down side is that when you come to finish the bowl, you are pretty much committed to the form you rough-turned months or years earlier.

Because the wood is easiest to work when freshly felled, the bulk of the waste can be removed very quickly. The wood is relatively soft and therefore cuts easily, though the surface remaining is not particularly smooth. As

Set of Bowls

A set of bowls is a very satisfying project to complete, especially if they're exactly the same height. (Show off by putting a straightedge across them.) When making a set of bowls or repeating a form in production, develop regular methods of work. Don't adjust any techniques halfway through because it will show. Save the new techniques for the next set.

MATERIAL: She-oak
SIZE: 7 in. by 2¾ in.
            (180mm by 65mm)

the wood dries, the fibers stiffen, which makes them easier to cut cleanly.

Rough-turning enables you to get the maximum from green logs that would otherwise split if left solid. A small tree—say 12 in. (300mm) in diameter—should yield bowls about ¾ in. to 1⅛ in. (20mm to 30mm) less in diameter. Similarly, dimensioned defect-free seasoned wood would likely come from a tree nearly twice the diameter. The moment a tree is felled it starts to dry out and split, so the sooner you can turn a log into rough bowls, the more you are likely to get from it.

Rough-turned bowls warp partly due to the wood drying and partly because of the altered stresses that occur when the center of the block is removed. I tend also to rough-turn bowls made from seasoned timber, mainly because a piece of walnut known to have been sawn at least 35 years previously warped on me, presumably after the tensions within the wood were altered by my hollowing it. If possible I'll let seasoned wood stand in its roughed-out form for at least 24 hours, although two to three hours is probably sufficient.

It is best to avoid any wood well known for warping; some timbers can move so much that it is impossible to obtain a bowl from the warped form. To test a wood, turn a small, thin bowl—it needn't be finished—and cook it in a microwave oven for one minute on full power or until it is too hot to handle. It should come out sizzling and steaming. If it is going to warp, it will do so while cooking or within a few minutes afterwards. Watch the bowl in the oven, and if you smell burning, switch the microwave off immediately. Those without microwave ovens can put the bowl over a heat source such as a stove or radiator for a few hours or in the hot sun.

Blanks for rough-turning need to be cut carefully to ensure that you get the best from your logs. Most of the problems that occur as the wood seasons occur because the grain is unevenly balanced. If your blanks are of even density, that is, all burl, all fiddleback, or all plain and even grain, you should have few problems with distortion during drying, as the bowl goes slightly crinkly or slightly oval or both.

I store my rough-turned bowls in boxes for as long as possible. Each is dated so I know when it was turned.

SEASONING ROUGHED BOWLS

For the first few days of seasoning, I leave the roughed bowls in a loose pile, out of the sun and strong drafts but where air can circulate gently around all the surfaces. Usually I lean some on edge against a wall with others piled on top. Once the surface has dried, I toss them into large boxes, as shown in the photo on the facing page, where they sit for as long as possible. I'm thinking years here, not months, so it's a good idea to date each bowl so you know when you roughed it. I put the month and year.

A serious bowl turner will have many hundreds of bowls drying at any one time. And while you can easily tie up a lot of time and money in stock this way, it should be a good investment and better than money in the bank in the long run. I periodically check all my rough-turned bowls, transferring each to a different box, so what was on the bottom gets its turn on top. In this way I keep a check on mildew, borers, and splits. I pull out bowls that are splitting and turn them straight away, the moisture content dictating exactly what kind of bowl I'll make. I check moisture using a small meter, but the date the bowl was roughed is usually as good a guide, working on the traditional air-drying formula.

I have never found that waxing or painting a bowl's end grain to prevent it splitting ever did more than delay the inevitable, so all my bowls season in the raw. If a bowl is going to split, the sooner the better. Besides its questionable effectiveness, coating blanks with wax results in waxed shavings on the floor, which makes the floor dangerously slick and slippery. When this happens, splash around water or sand or both.

MICROWAVE DRYING

Microwave drying has been much vaunted as an efficient method for drying rough-turned bowls, but I have found it far too slow and tedious. I have better things to do than watch

Eucalyptus Burl Bowls

Turned green, these very thin bowls were dried in a microwave oven on full power for 90 seconds. Not all woods will distort, but those that do, do so quickly, within minutes.

MATERIAL:	Eucalyptus burl
SIZES:	5½ in. (140mm) diameter, 4¾ in. (120mm) diameter

bowl blanks in an oven for hours on end, even if weighing them every so often breaks the monotony. But I do use the microwave oven to season very thin green-turned bowls in order to warp them quickly and dramatically (see the photo above).

Seasoning does take time, but it's worth the effort. If your finished bowls can remain stable through changes in climate and humidity, chances are they'll be cherished for decades or even centuries and not be tossed aside after a few years because they warped or split.

4 ROUGH-TURNING THE PROFILE

I always rough out bowls in two stages. First I turn the profile (the outside form) with the face that will be the top of the bowl toward the headstock. Then I remount the partly turned bowl for hollowing, gripping it by the foot.

The transformation of a seasoned blank to the profile of a small bowl ready for sanding can take well less than a minute. Turning green wood can be even faster. Once the blank is mounted, I typically shape a 10-in. (250mm) salad bowl in a few minutes. Consequently it is important to have simple, quick, and efficient ways of fixing a blank on the lathe and then equally simple ways of removing it. So before I discuss how to use the tools to best advantage at the roughing stage, let's look at the options for mounting your blanks.

Fixing a Blank on the Lathe

For rough-turning the profile, you can fix a blank on the lathe using a screw chuck, a faceplate, or a chuck, or you can mount it between centers. There are pros and cons for each method, and which you choose will depend

partly on the diameter and thickness of the blank, partly on whether the wood is evenly grained or off-balance, and then on the flatness or unevenness of the faces.

Ideally you want to grip the blank without tail-center support so that, with the face that will be the top of the bowl toward the headstock, you can work all around the profile from any angle without the tail center getting in the way. Most of the splits and defects you might want to eliminate will be on or near the outside of the blank, so with the blank aligned this way, you can eliminate everything you don't want, as well as adjust the overall proportions of the bowl as you work the profile. On occasions when you need tail-center support, you can still work all of the outside of the bowl except for the very center of the base.

SCREW CHUCKS

Screw faceplates (often referred to and marketed as screw chucks) have a single center screw to which blanks can be attached on the lathe. Most modern chucks convert to a screw chuck.

For speed and efficiency when mounting bowl blanks, it's hard to beat a screw chuck, shown in use in the photo at right on the facing page. I regard these as essential tools for any

For speed and efficiency when mounting bowl blanks,
it's hard to beat a screw chuck.

A range of screw chucks enables you to provide optimum support for a blank.

A small blank can be held on a very short screw, here about ⅜ in. (9mm) long.

bowl turner—I have three and also an engineer's chuck with a coach bolt seen to the rear in the photo above. Both of the chucks in front have a reversible collar that gives each three diameters for the optimum support of a blank. Each face of these chucks has a tiny bead at the rim that a blank seats against more securely than against a flat face. The wider a faceplate is the better it grips and the greater support it can offer with a shorter screw. You should use the widest face your blank will allow (see the illustration on p. 64).

All commercial screws are at least 1 in. (25mm) long, which is typically far more than you need. Small blanks can usually be gripped on little more than ¼ in. (6mm), so I have a series of scrapwood discs seen to the front in the photo at left above to reduce the effective length of the screw. If the screw fails to grip, simply remove one disc.

A handy variation of the screw center is a lag bolt set in a three-jaw engineer's chuck. The bolt can be moved in and out to vary the effective length of the screw or be changed to one larger. If a blank spins on one screw, you simply

FACEPLATES AND LEVERAGE

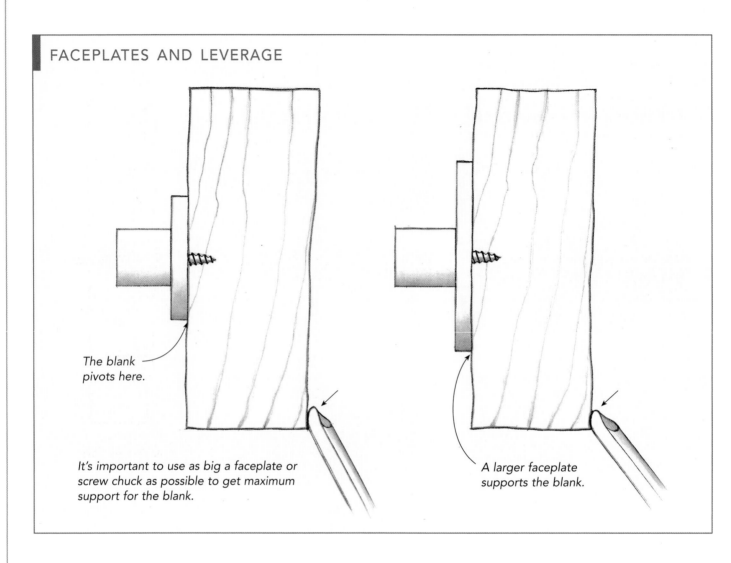

The blank pivots here.

It's important to use as big a faceplate or screw chuck as possible to get maximum support for the blank.

A larger faceplate supports the blank.

The Glaser screw (left) with it's finely machined thread is vastly superior to the copy (right), typical of many offered as a chuck accessory.

transfer the blank to another. The three jaws always provide a firm backing for the blank, but they're hazardous and can be painful if you catch your knuckles on them.

Traditionally, turners made their own screw faceplates, attaching a disc to a standard faceplate and fixing a large screw at center, as shown in the illustration on the facing page. They work well, and if they get damaged or worn, it's easy to make another. I replaced mine only when Jerry Glaser introduced his screw chuck with its hardened stainless-steel screw and parallel shank seen to the left in the photo at left. This screw has been much copied—the screw shown to the right is typical—but rarely emulated. I use

MAKING A SCREW CHUCK

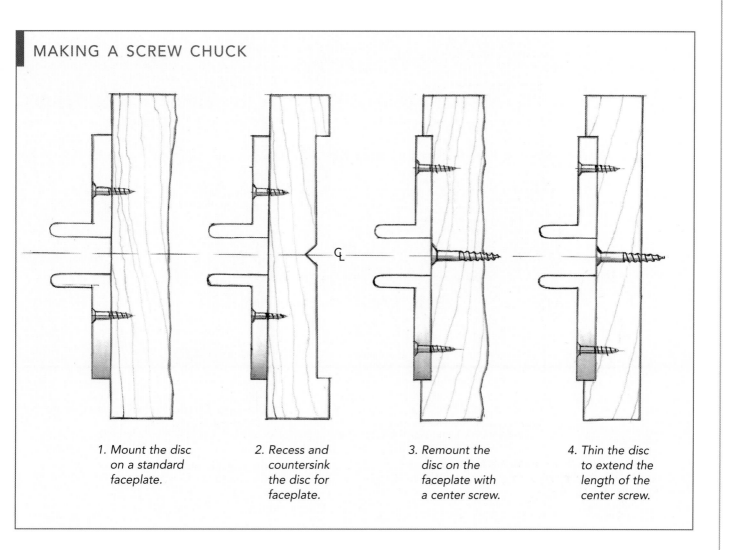

1. Mount the disc on a standard faceplate.

2. Recess and countersink the disc for faceplate.

3. Remount the disc on the faceplate with a center screw.

4. Thin the disc to extend the length of the center screw.

a Glaser screw to grip all my blanks, including those 66-lb. (30kilo) chunks for which I also use tail-center support.

Most commercial chucks come with a 2-in. (50mm) jaw set that converts to a screw faceplate with a long center screw. These are fine for small blanks up to 6 in. (150mm) in diameter but next to useless for larger and heavier blanks, when the small jaws cannot offer enough support or grip, no matter how long the screw. Tail-center support can keep the wood spinning true on the axis as you cut, but chances are that the screw will spin in a heavy chunk of wood and you'll need to transfer to a standard faceplate. You can broaden the face of

the chuck in screw faceplate mode by making a washer as shown in the photo at left on p. 66, but a dedicated screw faceplate is better.

There are two ways of getting a blank on a screw chuck, and each requires that you drill a pilot hole the diameter of the screw shank in the center of the flat face of a blank. (If you use a compass to mark out your blanks, there will be a deep pinprick at center.) If the face of the blank is less than flat and the blank is rocking on the screw, causing difficulties in cutting, use tail-center support to keep the blank spinning true. This keeps you from working all the base, and the tail center leaves a conical hole, so if you are mounting blanks and completing the

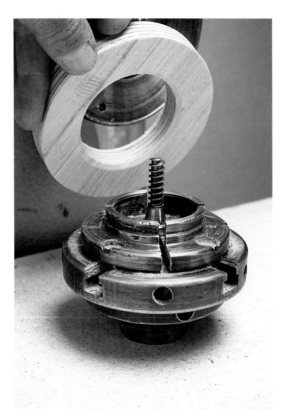

A turned washer broadens the face of a set of standard chuck jaws to provide a better grip for blanks above 6 in. (150mm) in diameter.

Heavy blanks are easiest to mount with the lathe running just fast enough to feed the screw into the center hole.

bowl profile (rather than just roughing out the form), ensure that the face of the blank is flat so it seats securely against the faceplate and doesn't require tailstock support.

The safest way to mount a bowl blank on a screw faceplate is with the lathe turned off. Use the handwheel to rotate the screw chuck, as you offer the blank up to the screw with the other hand. It can be difficult to bring the blank tight against the faceplate, so lock the drive shaft and use both hands to complete the job.

A faster way of mounting blanks, much favored by professional turners, is with the lathe running. This is not a technique for novices to use at higher speeds, but you shouldn't have a problem if your lathe is running 300 rpm to 500 rpm. (A major advantage of having a variable-speed lathe is that you can easily drop

the speed to mount the blank, then increase it as required for the turning.) The blanks should be at least 6 in. (150mm) in diameter so they have enough weight for inertia to snug them against the chuck as the screw spins in. Hold the blank so that when the screw catches in the hole only your palm is in contact with the face of the blank. It's almost a throwing action. If you have a variable-speed unit, mounting with the lathe running is by far the easiest way to handle heavier blanks because the lathe does the work (see the photo above).

Very large and heavy blanks should be mounted with the lathe running just fast enough to feed the screw into the center hole. Lack of torque at very low revs will usually keep the screw from spinning the wood as you hold it, but a better technique is to switch the lathe

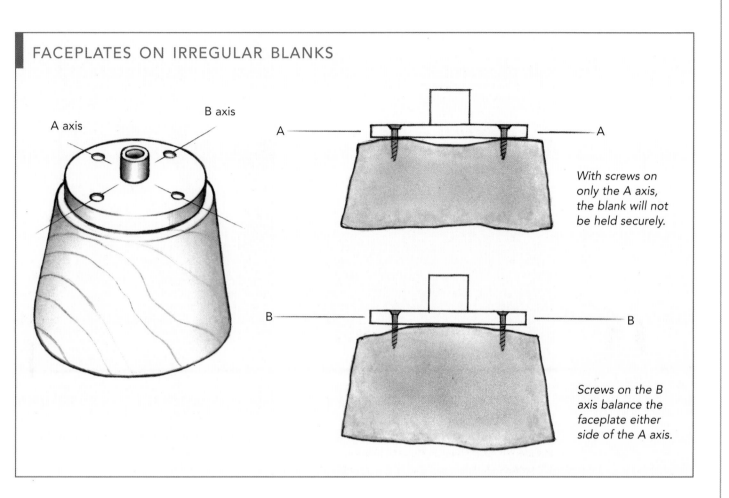

FACEPLATES ON IRREGULAR BLANKS

A axis

B axis

A ——————— A

With screws on only the A axis, the blank will not be held securely.

B ——————— B

Screws on the B axis balance the faceplate either side of the A axis.

off the moment the screw grabs the wood. For this you must have an "off" button you can nudge with your knee or hip. This is strictly a low-speed operation.

FACEPLATES

Faceplates are the flat metal discs that screw on to a drive spindle and come as standard with every lathe. Blanks are attached off the lathe by two or more screws, as shown in the photo at right, which makes faceplate mounting tedious when compared with screw chucks, especially on smaller bowls. Consequently I hardly ever use a faceplate anymore. However, they are better than a screw chuck for gripping uneven surfaces because screws can be inserted on either side of a high spot or axis, as shown in the illustration above.

A faceplate is the most secure way to hold a blank on the lathe.

Small blanks can be conveniently gripped in a chuck to shape most of the bowl's profile. You can complete the rim when you remount the blank for hollowing.

Expanding long-nose jaws within a drilled hole is a fast and simple way to grip a small blank.

Faceplates provide the most secure fixing for bowl blanks. Most come with four equally spaced screw holes, but you can easily drill more if you feel the need. In the days when I used faceplates, I seldom used more than two #14 wood screws penetrating the wood about ¾ in. to 1 in. (19mm to 25mm) on blanks up to 15 in. (380mm) in diameter. If the blank came loose as work proceeded, I'd stick in another couple of screws; if I had a massive catch, I'd just replace the screws with longer or fatter ones. During initial roughing cuts, you might want to bring up the tail center for extra support.

In general, you should place the screws across the grain so that if there is a split you've failed to notice—some are very difficult to spot—the wood is less likely to fly apart. Screws set along the grain sometimes cleave the wood. However, if you are intending to remount a

rough-turned bowl using the same screw holes, you should align the screws along the grain where movement is minimal as the wood shrinks.

CHUCKS

Chucks come in a variety of shapes and sizes, with a range of jaws. They are versatile and dependable, gripping either by clamping around a blank or by expanding within a hole drilled on a drill press or a recess turned on the lathe. In most situations, you'll cut a blank round on a bandsaw and grip it, but this is tedious when dealing with blanks smaller than 3 in. (75mm). For such small blanks, expanding within a hole in a square blank is faster.

A two-spur drive is preferable to a four-spur drive because it grips better on an uneven surface.

When working with small, round blanks, a chuck can be the most efficient method for holding the wood, as shown in the photo at left on the facing page. The obvious problem is that you cannot work the rim, but that portion can be easily turned true once the bowl is reversed for hollowing.

Mounting a blank by expanding the chuck jaws into a drilled hole provides a faster and more positive grip than a small screw chuck when working small or lightweight blanks. The hole needs to be only slightly larger than the chuck jaws, but of course the wider the hole the better because that provides more surface area. A flat-bit drill is the fastest way to drill a hole, but the spur can easily go too deep so I use a Forstner bit. If the blank doesn't sit square, slacken the jaws and adjust it by hand as shown in the photo at right on the facing page.

BETWEEN CENTERS

Blanks for natural-edged bowls such as those shown in the photo at right or that have a very uneven face are best rough-turned between centers. Such blanks are easily held between centers, and you can adjust the blank as needed to realign the grain patterns or rim of the bowl. As usual, you will need to turn a foot so you can remount the bowl for hollowing. You can work all but the very center of the base, and the remaining nub will easily break or chisel away.

A two-spur drive is preferable to a four-spur drive because it grips better on an uneven surface. Also, a two-spur drive can be located in a small V-groove that you can quickly chisel into the surface of your blank, to prevent it from spinning. Use a chisel the same width as your drive, as shown in the top left photo on p. 70.

Bark-rimmed bowls generally look best if the rim is balanced around a horizontal plane.

The two spurs allow the blank to be pivoted to either side for precise positioning of the tail center, as shown in the top right and bottom right photos on p. 70. Note how I use some part of the lathe, either the tool rest or the headstock, to steady my arm and the blank while positioning the tail center.

Natural-edged bowls with a bark rim tend to look better when the highest points of the rim are in the same horizontal plane, that is, the same height. Likewise, the lower points of the rim look better on the same lower horizontal plane, parallel to the plane of the upper points. Align the two-spur drive along the main axis of the bark or natural face. Orient the axis on which the upper points lie at 90 degrees to the lathe axis. To bring the lower points into a parallel plane, draw a line from the lowest point on the rim around the partly turned profile and compare the position of this line on the other side of the blank (see the bottom left and center

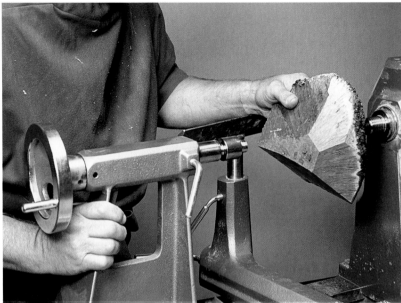

To mount a blank with an uneven surface between centers, chisel a V-groove to receive a two-spur drive (left). As you bring the tail center up, steady the blank by resting your arm on the tool rest (above).

On blanks with a symmetrical round face, align the two-spur drive along the main axis of the curve on top of the blank. Mount the blank with the top at 90 degrees to the lathe axis and the sides evenly balanced. A pencil line drawn on the roughed bowl profile indicates how much the blank needs to be repositioned to bring the lower portions of the rim into the same plane (left, center). Make this adjustment easier by using the lathe to support your arm as you pivot the blank on the two-spur drive (above).

photos on the facing page). Reposition the tail center until you can draw a line that touches both the lowest points of the rim.

For a more positive drive, you can use a spur faceplate, which is a variation of a two-prong drive. Make this by fixing bolts through two of the four holes in a standard faceplate so that about 1 in. (25mm) of bolt stands proud of the locking nuts. Then on a grinder sharpen the end of each bolt to a point.

You need to drill two holes in the blank to accept the bolts. The easiest way to locate the holes is to align the spur faceplate on the blank, then tap the bolt heads with a hammer to mark the wood.

Roughing the Profile

Ideally you want to be able to work all around the job, unhindered by a tail center, so you should try to mount blanks using either a faceplate or a screw chuck. Once the blank is fixed on the lathe, you should always spin it by hand before switching on the power. Partly this ensures that the blank spins freely and clear of the rest, but you need also to check the balance. A disc of evenly grained timber accurately fixed should present few problems.

If the blank is not centrally mounted or if the weight is unevenly distributed with dense grain in one portion and open grain elsewhere, one side will quickly gravitate toward the lathe bed. An off-balance blank will vibrate severely when run at high speed, so unbalanced blanks

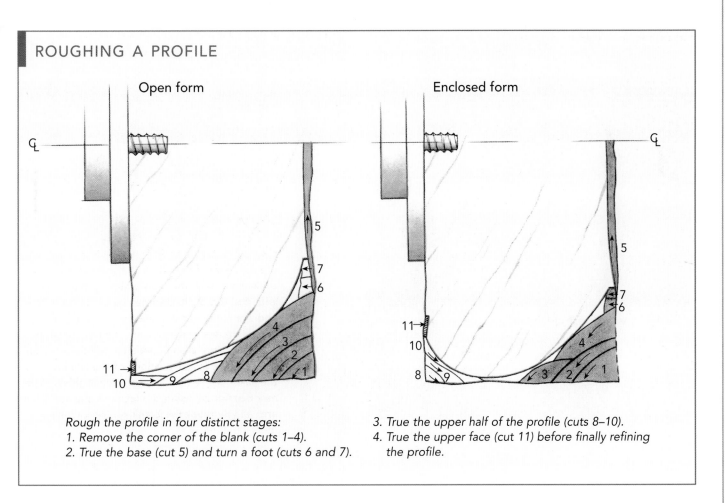

ROUGHING A PROFILE

Open form

Enclosed form

Rough the profile in four distinct stages:
1. Remove the corner of the blank (cuts 1–4).
2. True the base (cut 5) and turn a foot (cuts 6 and 7).

3. True the upper half of the profile (cuts 8–10).
4. True the upper face (cut 11) before finally refining the profile.

Using a Spur Faceplate

A shopmade spur faceplate can be used to mount an irregular turning. Inserting bolts through the holes of the faceplate provides a way to make a larger version of a spur chuck and grip larger workpieces.

2 Drill holes at the bolt marks the same diameter as the bolts ½ in. (13mm) deep.

1 Align the faceplate on the blank and drive each bolt into the wood.

3 Slide the tailstock into place to secure the blank against the drive.

The aim at this stage of making a bowl is to get the waste and defects away as quickly as possible while developing the approximate form.

must always be started at a low speed. Always err on the side of caution guided by the speed chart on p. 13. If you have an electronic speed control, get in the habit of adjusting the speed back toward zero before you switch on the lathe so it always starts slowly.

Initial cuts should aim to true the blank as quickly as possible, eliminating all flat areas and any defects or features you don't want in your final bowl. After that, you can assess what you have left and work toward your final shape. At this roughing stage, you need to allow as much leeway as possible for the bowl's final shape.

Approach the job in four distinct stages, as shown in the illustration on p. 71. On traditionally shaped bowls, start by removing the corners of the blank to reduce any eccentric weight (cuts 1 through 4), then true the base (cut 5) and turn a foot (cuts 6 and 7). Third, true the upper half of the profile (cuts 8 through 10) and, fourth, true the upper face where the rim will be (cut 11) before finally refining the profile. Truing the upper face is not vital because you might want to keep it for the texture, but it will make it easier to remount the bowl accurately for hollowing.

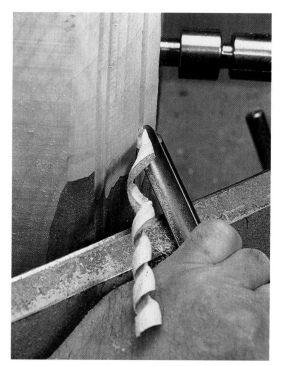

In a pulling shear cut, the gouge should be rolled over about 45 degrees and tilted up about 35 degrees from horizontal so the portion of the edge cutting is presented at about 45 degrees to the oncoming wood.

CUTTING TECHNIQUES

In bowl blanks, the grain runs across the face of the blank and at 90 degrees to the lathe axis, so all cuts should be made from smaller to larger diameters and in from either face to shear-cut the grain cleanly.

Both green and seasoned timber are turned using the same techniques. Most woods work

more readily when green, and as the sap sprays out, you, and anything else in line, will get wet and possibly stained. Woods full of tannin such as oak or walnut will blacken your hands and stain your clothing, so don't wear your Sunday best. When working very fresh wood, I wear full waterproofs. Stained hands are best cleaned using lemon juice or one of the commercially available hand cleansers containing citric acid.

A tool is easier to control if you keep your weight behind it. Have the handle against your side and move with it as the cut proceeds.

The aim at this stage of making a bowl is to get the waste and defects away as quickly as possible while developing the approximate form. The quality of the surface is not paramount, so the best cuts at first are pulling shear cuts (see the photos on p. 73 and above, which remove a great deal of wood while leaving a grooved surface and some torn end grain.

You can use either deep-fluted or shallow gouges to rough out the profile but not scrapers, which are slow to use and typically leave a very rough surface. When working close to the rest, I always use the shortest gouges I have that can do the job, saving the longer tools for working well over the rest when hollowing. Gouges are expensive, so there's no point in using up valuable steel when you don't have to. A ½-in. (13mm) gouge will cope with most profile roughing cuts, but I favor a shallow tool (typically sold as a spindle or detail gouge for center-work) because the shaving gets away faster than from a deep-fluted gouge. Wet shavings can jam in a deep flute, slowing the flow of work.

For blanks in excess of 12 in. (305mm) in diameter, I use a ⁹⁄₁₆-in. (15mm) half-round or ⅝-in. (16mm) gouge. Do not be tempted into using the larger square-nosed gouges commonly found in sets of turning tools and designed for roughing spindles between centers. These are not designed for turning bowls and are consequently very inefficient and can be the source of spectacular catches you'd rather not experience.

In a pulling shear cut, the gouge is rolled over about 45 degrees as shown in the photo on p. 73. The bevel need not rub, but in the photo at left note that the tool is tilted up about 35 degrees from horizontal so the portion of the edge cutting is presented at about 45 degrees to the oncoming wood. I have my right hand near the ferrule and the end of the handle against my side. As the cut proceeds, I keep my weight behind the tool by keeping the handle against my side and moving with it.

Begin the cut with the tool on its side and pivot the edge through an arc into the wood. You always gain the most control bringing an edge in to cut by swinging the edge through an arc (so the tool pivots on the rest), rather than pushing it forward (see the illustration on the facing page). With the tool on its side you'll take only a small shaving. To get a fatter shaving, you need to rotate the edge very slightly clockwise as you simultaneously drop the tool handle to pitch the edge up. This compound movement should produce a shaving like that in the photo on p. 73.

Whenever you bring a tool in to begin cutting, you always have to adjust the angle of the edge to the oncoming wood until you obtain the best shaving. With practice you do this in a fraction of a second because you know from experience what size and type of shaving you should be getting. From timbers such as ash, cherry, and walnut, you can obtain long, curly shavings, whereas the shorter-grained burls typi-

ROUGHING CUTS USING A GOUGE

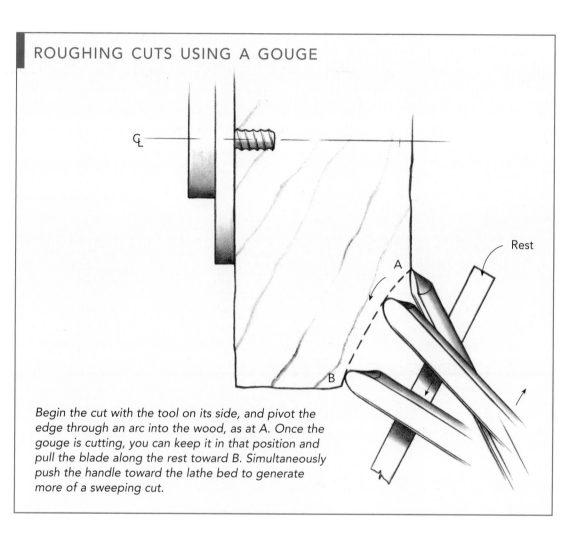

Rest

A

B

C̸L

Begin the cut with the tool on its side, and pivot the edge through an arc into the wood, as at A. Once the gouge is cutting, you can keep it in that position and pull the blade along the rest toward B. Simultaneously push the handle toward the lathe bed to generate more of a sweeping cut.

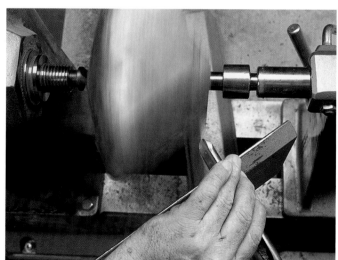

When you are turning more space than wood, be especially careful to take the edge through an arc into the wood, pivoting it on the rest rather than pushing it forward.

A pulling arcing cut removes waste quickly in the upper part of the profile.

For a thrusting shear cut, bring the handle near horizontal and rub the bevel on the wood as you push the tool forward. Stop just short of the rim to avoid splintering the grain.

cally produce more chips and dust. Once the gouge is cutting, you can keep it in that position and pull it toward you and along the rest, simultaneously pushing the handle slightly toward the lathe bed to generate more of a sweeping cut as you shape the bowl's profile.

When a blank is very rough and you are turning more space than wood, as shown in the photos on p. 75, swing the edge through a series of arcs until the blank is turned true.

To true the upper portion of the blank, you need to adjust the rest. You can continue using the same pulling, arcing cuts in series, as shown in the top photos on the facing page. But often it is more convenient to bring the handle nearer the horizontal for a thrusting shear cut, with the tool pointing in the direction you're going (see the bottom photos on the facing page). In these four photos, you'll see two standard grips, each of which is acceptable, although a hand-over grip (top photos) allows you to control where the shavings go.

Remember to stop short of the top face to keep the rim from splintering. The ability to move smoothly from one cutting technique to another is a very enjoyable aspect of turning wood, and without much practice you can learn to raise the tool handle at the end of the pulling cut so that the edge comes down (the handle moving up) and the tool points in the direction you're cutting in one fluid movement, as shown in the illustration at right. Then you can steer the tool around the rest of the curve, stopping just short of the rim.

Pushing the tool rather than pulling it gives you more control cutting curves. On a smaller outflowing form, such as that shown in the top photo on p. 78, this is the best technique for establishing a good profile.

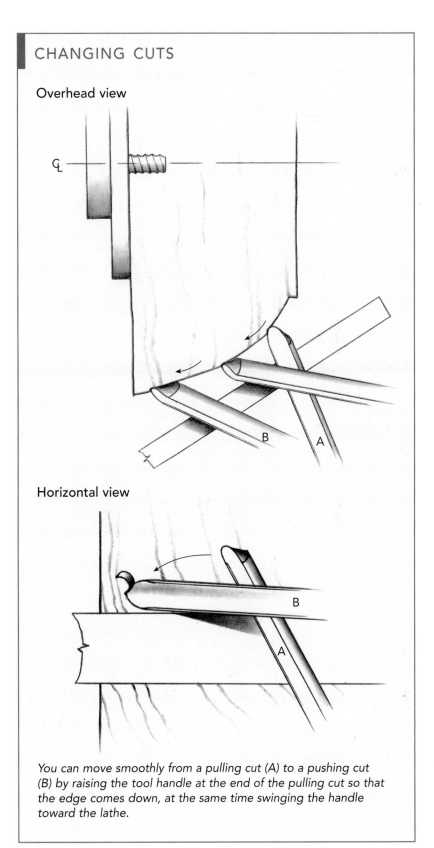

CHANGING CUTS

Overhead view

Horizontal view

You can move smoothly from a pulling cut (A) to a pushing cut (B) by raising the tool handle at the end of the pulling cut so that the edge comes down, at the same time swinging the handle toward the lathe.

A thrusting cut using a deep-fluted gouge is effective on smaller out-flowing bowls because the lower edge can take a wide shaving while you steer the tool around the curve.

Always cut in from the top face to keep the rim from splintering.

On burls where there's no particular direction, you can usually cut toward the headstock and get a clean surface while watching the profile develop on the top horizon of the form. Here I decide to keep the mass around the rim for possible beading.

As you turn the upper section of a bark-rimmed or natural-edge bowl, there is always a problem with the rim splitting away when cutting from the smaller to larger diameter. During the roughing process, as with a normal blank, cut in from the rim so the bark portions are always supported by layers of wood below.

To cut in from the top face of the blank on an enclosed form, use a pull cut, mirroring the roughing cuts in the lower half of the profile (see the bottom left photo on the facing page). On burls where the wood has no particular direction, you can typically cut toward the headstock as shown in the bottom right photo on the facing page. Here I decide to keep the mass around the rim for possible beading.

On cylindrical forms, you should cut in from each face.

At the roughing stage, you don't always need to true the top face (the rim of the bowl) unless it's particularly rough. You might even want to retain the surface for a character-filled rim in the final bowl. However, if you need to true the rim, as you might to establish precise dimensions on a dry blank when you'll complete the profile in one go, have the tool on its side mirroring the initial roughing cuts (see the photo at left below). Larger amounts of wood can be removed from an upper face using a shear cut toward center, as shown in the photo at right below.

To true the top face, have the flute facing the wood, with the gouge rolled over about 45 degrees.

For serious waste removal on a face, use a strong deep-fluted gouge for a shear cut toward center.

Tasmanian Myrtle Bowl

I try to avoid straight lines, so the upper portion of this basically cylindrical form is asymmetrically curved. The understated ogee of the lower portion meets the slightly concave upper portion to form a well-defined angle.

MATERIAL: Tasmanian myrtle
SIZE: 6⅝ in. by 4¼ in.
(170mm by 110mm)

Turn away only as much as is required to eliminate a defect.

ELIMINATING DEFECTS

It frequently happens that your blanks will contain bark, splits, or some other defect that you don't want in your bowls. As you eliminate these, it is very easy to reduce the size of the blank far more than you need. You've paid for all of the blank, so you might as well try to maintain its maximum dimensions. And if you're selling your bowls, remember that any reduction in either the height or width will typically result in a lower price. Many of my bowls with wide, thin rims, like that shown in the photo at right on p. 166, emerged from blanks where I had to remove a major defect below the rim.

Turn away only as much as is required to eliminate the defect. With bark, define its top and bottom by pencil lines, as shown in the photo below, then remove as little as possible between the lines until it's gone. If instead you want to keep the bark, bear in mind that later it might flake away and that the bowl wall needs to be thick enough to remain whole (rather than hole) in that eventuality.

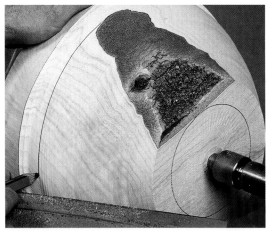

Mark the extremities of any defect you want to remove, in this case the bark, then work between those lines, taking care not to remove more than is absolutely necessary.

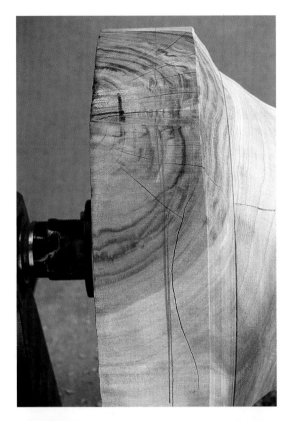

I turn away the big crack lying within the two lines (left) before noting the remaining end-grain splits on the freshly cut surface (below). I don't touch these until the upper part of the profile is determined (bottom left). From here the final rough profile (bottom right) is only a few pull cuts away.

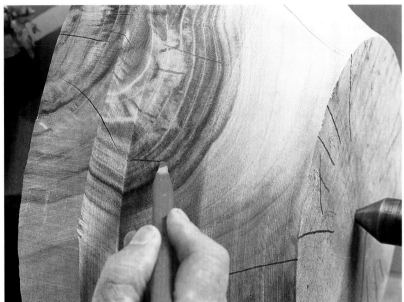

It can be very difficult to find the extent of some splits, so mark their position on the face of the blank, then when you come to check the surface, you know exactly the area to look. In the photos on p. 81, I turn away the big crack lying within the two lines before marking out the remaining end-grain splits on the freshly cut surface. I don't touch these until the upper part of the profile is determined. From here the final rough profile is only a few pull cuts away.

This will leave you with some pretty odd-looking potential bowls, but even if you need to remove the bulk of the lower half of the blank, there will still be some fine outflowing forms in what you have left, like that shown in the top left photo on p. 179.

Preparation for Hollowing

Before you're done with the bowl in its first fixing, you must know how you're going to remount it for hollowing. The most convenient way of holding a bowl for hollowing is by grip-ping a foot. But if you have only small-diameter jaws, these could be too small for a properly sized foot on a larger bowl. In that case, a recess in the base into which the jaws can expand is more secure. Alternatively you can use a face-plate or screw chuck. The disadvantage here is that you eventually have a screw hole or holes to fill or eliminate by re-turning the base (see chapter 8 to see what this involves).

The quickest and easiest grip is provided by chuck jaws contracting around a foot, but for very heavy work using solid stock (as opposed to gum-streaked or less-than-solid burl) a faceplate and screws are a more secure option. Whichever method you use, the aim is to support as wide an area as possible. Using a contracting grip or faceplate not only supports the widest diameter but also, if the rough-turned bowl warps dra-matically during seasoning, you can flatten the base and grip what remains of the foot fairly easily. To accommodate warping, a recess needs to be deeper than the sufficient ⅛ in. (3mm) to ³⁄₁₆ in. (5mm), and this can lead to design

To turn the base, begin by truing its rim, squeezing the tool edge against the wood. Then roll the tool and bring the bevel onto the smooth surface just cut for a shear cut to center.

problems later. If at all possible, grip a foot or short tenon rather than have the jaws expanding into a recess.

On a roughed bowl, the foot needs to be very slightly dovetailed for the most secure grip. And always err on the side of having the foot a little large rather than too small. You can always reduce the diameter later. And don't make it too thin—although most chuck jaws will grip on as little as ⅛ in. (3mm), you do have to allow for warping.

The base needs to be slightly concave so it seats flat against either the chuck jaws or faceplate. If the base is in anyway convex, it will be difficult to fix accurately in a chuck or on a faceplate.

To turn the base, first true its rim, as shown in the photo at left on the facing page, by squeezing the tool edge against the wood until the tick-tick sound becomes smooth. Now the rim is true. Roll the tool and bring the bevel on to this smooth surface, and take a shear cut to center (see the photo at right on the facing page). Aim to make the bottom of the base flat, then take a last pass, dishing it slightly. Remember that the shallow gouge is never used flute up for facework: It catches every time!

To shape the foot, use a fingernail-ground shallow gouge. Have the bevel aligned in the direction you want to cut, with the tool on its side (flute facing away from the wood) and the handle dropped about 20 degrees below horizontal. Keeping the tool pinned firmly to the rest, raise the handle to pivot the edge down through an arc into the wood. The moment the nose of the tool is in the wood, the bevel should be riding the surface just cut, giving support to the edge as the cut proceeds.

For a better shaving, rotate the tool very slightly clockwise, as shown in the photo at right. Be careful; if you rotate too far, the wood will bear down on the unsupported edge and you'll have a catch. For much the same reason, at the end of the cut, where the sweep of the

To cut a foot, use a shallow fingernail-ground gouge on its side, with the bevel aligned in the direction of the cut.

profile meets the foot, you need to bring the tool onto its side again so the profile doesn't bear down on and catch the left side of the edge. Having cut the foot, you can pivot the tool on its nose and drop the handle so you shift to the pulling shear cut you started with. And remember to taper the foot slightly to produce a dovetail shape if you're intending to mount the foot in a chuck. This is as difficult a cut as you'll have to make: Now is the time to practice.

To prepare the base for rechucking on a screw chuck, drill a hole at center while the bowl is on the lathe. The most precise method is to mount a twist drill in the tailstock so you can wind the drill in to the right depth for the screw chuck. Avoid drills with an extended point and don't make the hole any deeper than you have to. A faster method, which I prefer although it produces a less precisely sized hole,

IDEAL FOOT FOR RECHUCKING

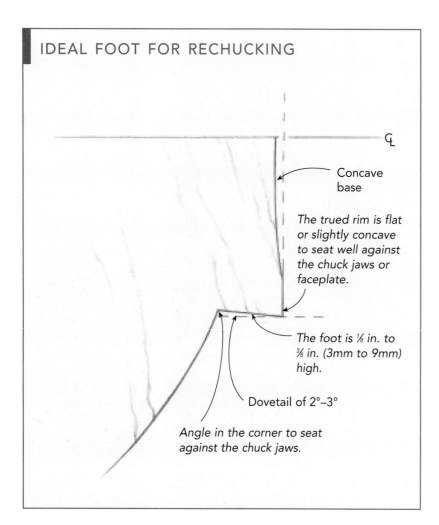

C̵L

Concave base

The trued rim is flat or slightly concave to seat well against the chuck jaws or faceplate.

The foot is ⅛ in. to ⅜ in. (3mm to 9mm) high.

Dovetail of 2°–3°

Angle in the corner to seat against the chuck jaws.

Mark out the base for faceplate mounting. Drill screw holes where the circle (corresponding to the diameter of the hole position in your faceplate) intersects the line drawn through center.

ROUGHING THE INSIDE FROM THE LEFT

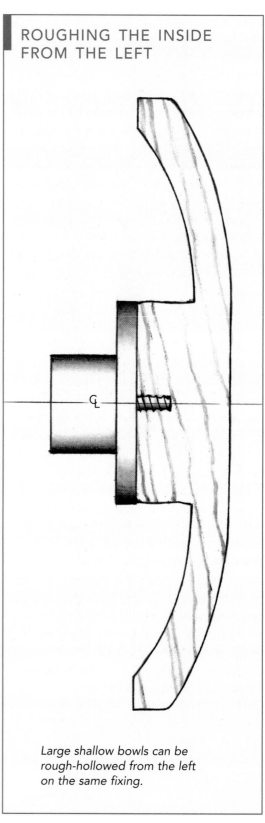

C̵L

Large shallow bowls can be rough-hollowed from the left on the same fixing.

is to drill by hand using a twist drill in a handle (see the photo on p. 89).

To lay out the holes for a faceplate, mark center and the diameter on which the holes are located. Then draw a line through center to intersect the circle and drill holes for the screws at the intersections (see the photo on the facing page). I use a pump-action drill for accuracy and to ensure I don't go too deep. If you are turning green wood and will need to use the same screw holes later to remount the bowl for completion, place the holes along the grain where shrinkage will be minimal.

For years I remounted bowls for completion on two #14 wood screws penetrating the wood about ⁷⁄₁₆ in. (12mm). I preferred using two screws rather than a single one at center because I could make the bottom of the bowl slightly thinner. When I did hit a screw, I could repair the hole to look like a knot. The wider the faceplate, the better support you have for the bowl and the shorter the screws you can use. A bowl that is 6 in. by 3 in. (150mm by 75mm) can be held on a ⅜-in. (9mm) screw easily, provided the faceplate is at least one-third the diameter.

On very large and shallow bowls, you can begin rough-hollowing, leaving a boss the diameter of the screw chuck at center, as shown in the illustration at right on the facing page. When it's time to remount the bowl to finish the profile, you can rechuck on the same screw or grip the boss with a chuck (see chapter 6 for how to turn off the boss).

If you are working with a dry blank, you'll complete the profile now and need to know about finishing cuts (see p. 111 for "Final Decisions Concerning the Profile").

Rounded-Based Bowls

With slightly rounded bases, these bowls can wobble gently but never tip over. Rim detail relieves the otherwise stark forms.

MATERIAL: Tasmanian myrtle

SIZE: 7½ in. by 4 in. (190mm by 100mm)

5 ROUGH-HOLLOWING

When you remount a bowl for hollowing, having rough-turned the profile, most of the basic design decisions have been made and the shape established. You should hollow the bowl as soon as possible after you have turned the profile, especially when working green wood. If you have to delay the process more than 30 minutes, wrap the partly turned

bowl in plastic or bury it in its shavings and keep it out of direct sunlight and drafts. For longer delays, put the bowl in a plastic bag with damp shavings. The idea is to keep the surface from losing moisture while the blank is solid and thus prevent splits from developing.

During a rough-turning session, I typically work through an hour's worth of blanks at a time. So I cut the discs, then turn the profiles, heaping shavings over the partly turned bowls until they are hollowed. This method of work provides opportunities to focus and to vary my activity during the hour, which is good for me mentally and physically, but it also limits the possibility that the bowls will split on me as I work.

During initial hollowing, the idea is to remove the center as quickly and efficiently as possible, leaving the wall thick enough so that even after the form warps during the seasoning process, you can still complete the bowl. With most woods, the ideal wall thickness for seasoning a rough-turned bowl is about 10 percent of the diameter. Thus a 10-in. (25mm)-diameter bowl should have an even wall thickness of 1 in. (25mm) or slightly more. If you need the thicker rims and heavier walls required for some woods like the red gum shown in the

Red gum bowls. Some burls with heavy bark intrusions and big gum veins are best worked thick so they are less likely to fly apart.

Rough-hollowing is a speedy process. A 6-in. (150mm)-diameter bowl should take about six cuts.

Nests of roughed bowls. Common in production turning for centuries when work was done on reciprocal pole lathes, coring multiple bowls from a single blank is once again a viable technique, thanks to several effective coring systems on the market.

photo on the facing page, think in terms of 15 percent or even 25 percent of the diameter.

Rough-hollowing a bowl, especially when the wood is green, should be a speedy process, with small bowls up to 6 in. (150mm) in diameter requiring only about six cuts using a ½-in. (13mm) deep-fluted bowl gouge. A 12-in. (305mm) bowl should take a couple of minutes. I'm talking about rough-hollowing here, not turning the inside to completion. I don't want to terrify novices with unreasonable expectations, but you need to know where you're heading (even if you don't get there). It's like climbing Everest: The view gets better the higher you go.

These days it is common practice to use one of the bowl-nesting systems to save and make

use of the inside of the bowl. Typically a 12-in. by 4-in. (100mm by 305mm) bowl blank will yield at least three bowls as shown in the photo above or provide a cone for some other project. With the right wood in the right condition, you can remove the inside of a bowl as roughed bowls in much the same time that it takes to hollow the form using a gouge. However, before discussing how to salvage the inside of a bowl, let's consider remounting the blank for hollowing and then how gouges and scrapers are used to remove the inside.

Remounting the Bowl for Hollowing

If the wood is of even density and you have turned the foot correctly with a flat or slightly concave bottom and a crisp angle where the foot meets the bowl profile, your partly turned bowl should seat in the chuck jaws accurately and

If the remounted bowl is more than a little off center, you should true up the upper profile before proceeding with work on the face or hollowing.

run true. However, it often happens that one jaw will bite into the wood more than the others and pull the job slightly off center. If you are using a faceplate and screws, the chances of the partly turned bowl running absolutely true are remote.

If the bowl is barely off center, it's no big deal at this stage, and I'd not bother to true it up. Greater eccentricity, however, leads to vibration at higher speeds and a more uneven wall thickness in the seasoning bowl, so you need to true the profile before embarking on the face and hollowing cuts. If necessary for safety, use tail-center support. To true the upper portion of the profile, take a series of light cuts to remove the surplus wood. Follow the general rule of cutting from smaller to larger diameter.

Truing the face involves the same procedure as truing the base of the bowl (see the photos on p. 82) or any other flat surface. You can use either a shallow or a deep-fluted gouge; the former gives you a better view of what is happen-

True the rim by squeezing the edge against the wood, then rub the bevel on the trued surface for a shear cut in to center.

ing since the upper wing of the latter obscures your vision. First, squeeze the edge against the rotating wood until the tick-tick sound stops, indicating that the surface is smooth (see the bottom left photo on the facing page). Then roll the tool over so the bevel rides that smooth surface and take a shear cut into center (see the photo at right on the facing page).

Hollowing

Once the face is trued and turned flat (and you should check this with a straightedge), measure the height of the bowl or eyeball it and drill a depth hole at center. You can do this with a drill mounted in the tail center, but it's faster to drill by hand using a twist drill in a handle as shown in the photo below. If there is no hole at center (typically there is if you use a screw chuck), create a pilot hole for the drill using a small gouge. To start the drilling, bring the drill bevel to ride on the side of the hole before rais-

ing the handle and pushing the drill gently into the wood. I have a number of marks ground on my depth drill and I work in relation to those, although you might find a stop or masking tape a more accurate gauge. For tool junkies, both depth drills and measuring gauges are available commercially.

The advantage of drilling the hole is twofold. First, the bottom of the hole defines the depth to which you should hollow. Second, it makes the end of the cut into center much easier because you no longer need the precision required when working solid wood; the catches that occur when you push the gouge too aggressively into and across center are less likely.

Once the depth hole is drilled, you can use either gouges or scrapers to remove the waste. Gouges are generally faster, less likely to catch, and altogether a more elegant way of doing the job. Scrapers require a more delicate touch but can be a better option for some very hard woods that require frequent regrinding of the tool. I

To drill a depth hole, eyeball the required depth and work in relation to a mark you make on your drill. To start the drill, rest the bevel on the edge of the screw hole at center, then raise the handle and simultaneously push the tool forward.

I gain most control of the tool by holding the tool with my right hand on or very near the ferrule, aligning my forearm with the handle.

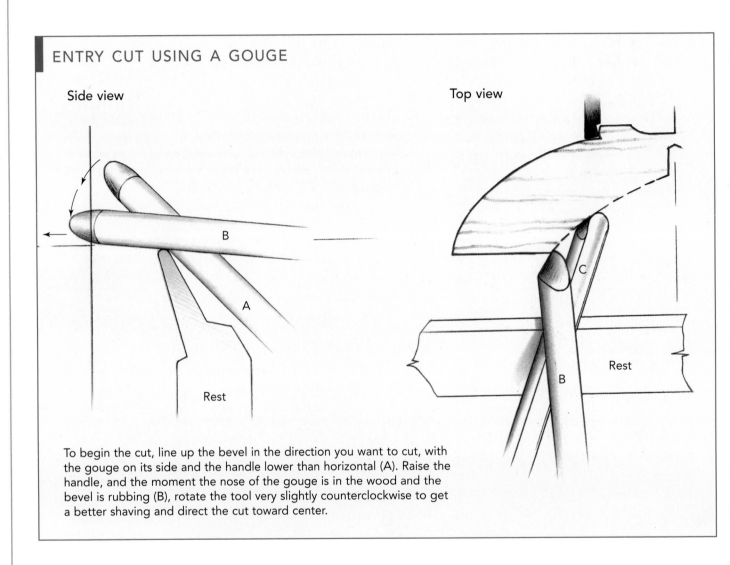

ENTRY CUT USING A GOUGE

Side view

Top view

Rest

Rest

To begin the cut, line up the bevel in the direction you want to cut, with the gouge on its side and the handle lower than horizontal (A). Raise the handle, and the moment the nose of the gouge is in the wood and the bevel is rubbing (B), rotate the tool very slightly counterclockwise to get a better shaving and direct the cut toward center.

recall turning some batches of teak and rose-wood where I kept the grinder running and touched up the tool edge every few seconds. When I am regrinding so often, I prefer to reduce the length of a less expensive scraper than any gouge costing twice as much.

HOLLOWING WITH GOUGES

Deep-fluted gouges are designed for hollowing bowls and are preferable to shallow gouges, which tend to flex when cutting more than 2 in. (50mm) over the rest.

To begin the cut, have the tool on its side, the flute facing center, and line up the bevel in the direction you want to cut. The gouge tends

For the most efficient hollowing cut, hold the tool almost horizontally, with the flute rolled over, so that while the nose cuts cleanly, the right wing removes the waste as a nice fat shaving.

to kick away from center because the rotating wood bears down on the unsupported portion of the edge, so you need to have either a finger or the heel of your hand planted firmly on the rest to prevent the kickback. Start with the handle dropped below horizontal, then bring the edge in to cut through an arc by raising the handle, as shown in the illustration at left on the facing page.

As the nose of the gouge enters the wood, it must be on its side. The moment the nose is in the wood and the bevel is rubbing, rotate the tool very slightly counterclockwise and direct the cut toward center, as shown in the illustration at right on the facing page. Beware of rotating too far because a catch is always lurking, waiting to grab the upper wing of the edge.

For cuts on the upper portion of an enclosed form, you need a gouge with a long bevel so you can present the tool at a reasonable angle, as shown in the bottom photo at right and the photo at left on p. 92. If the bevel is steep, the handle lies too far across the bed and is difficult to hold firmly. You get better support for the tool if the rest is at right angles to the direction of the cut. As the cut proceeds around the

A long bevel makes the entry cut on the top half of an enclosed form easy.

curve toward the base as shown in the photo at right on p. 92, transfer to a gouge with a steeper bevel in order to maintain bevel contact with the wood.

I find I gain most control of the tool by holding the tool with my right hand on or very near the ferrule, aligning my forearm with the handle. With this grip, any tendency for the tool to

As you reach over the lathe bed to undercut the rim of a small enclosed form, get as much support as possible from the lathe and lever yourself off it as you bring the handle toward yourself.

As your cuts round the bend and head for center, transfer to a gouge with a steep bevel, which can rub the wood all the way across the bottom.

ROUGH-HOLLOWING CUTS

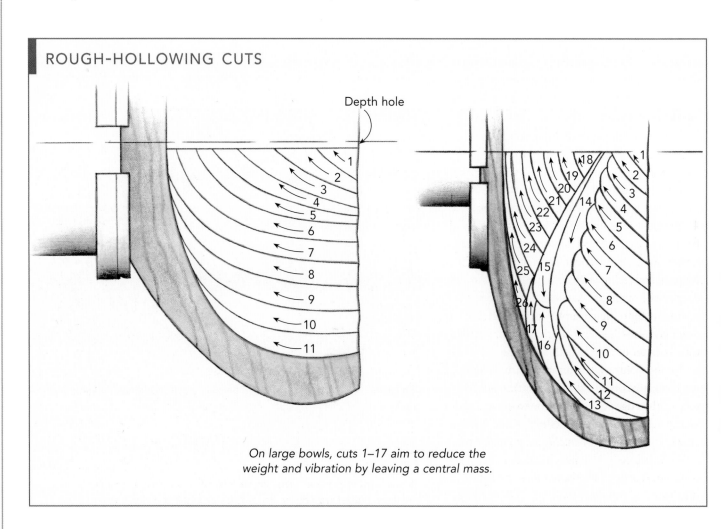

On large bowls, cuts 1–17 aim to reduce the weight and vibration by leaving a central mass.

PIVOTING HOLLOWING CUTS

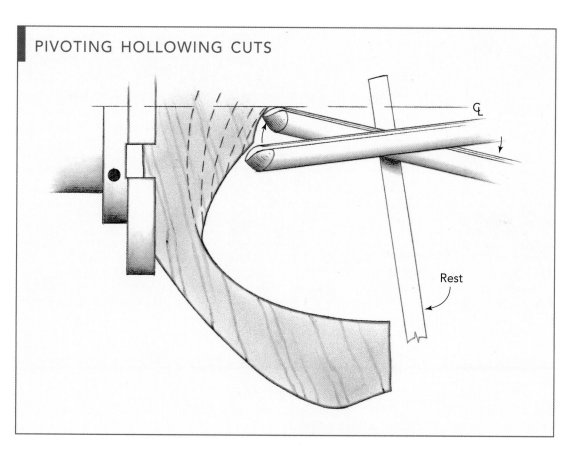

Rest

catch can largely be absorbed by my upper arm and shoulder. As soon as I am able, I bring my arm into my side for greater support.

As the gouge cuts, the nose lies at about 45 degrees to the oncoming wood, slicing the fibers as the right wing lifts away the shaving rather like a plough shear. Note in the illustrations on the facing page how the early cuts deepen the opening, with any force directed as near parallel to the lathe axis as possible. All the other cuts are directed toward the area within the diameter of the fixing.

For less controlled but rapid waste removal, I use the gouge on its side and pivoting on the rest, so the edge swings into the wood in a series of arcs, as shown in the illustration above. It's akin to rowing, except that I also push the fulcrum nearer center on larger bowls, making it a compound action. The bevel doesn't contact the wood.

When cutting uneven rims, be sure to take the tool firmly on a predetermined trajectory, regardless of what is or isn't there.

HOLLOWING AN ENCLOSED FORM USING A SCRAPER

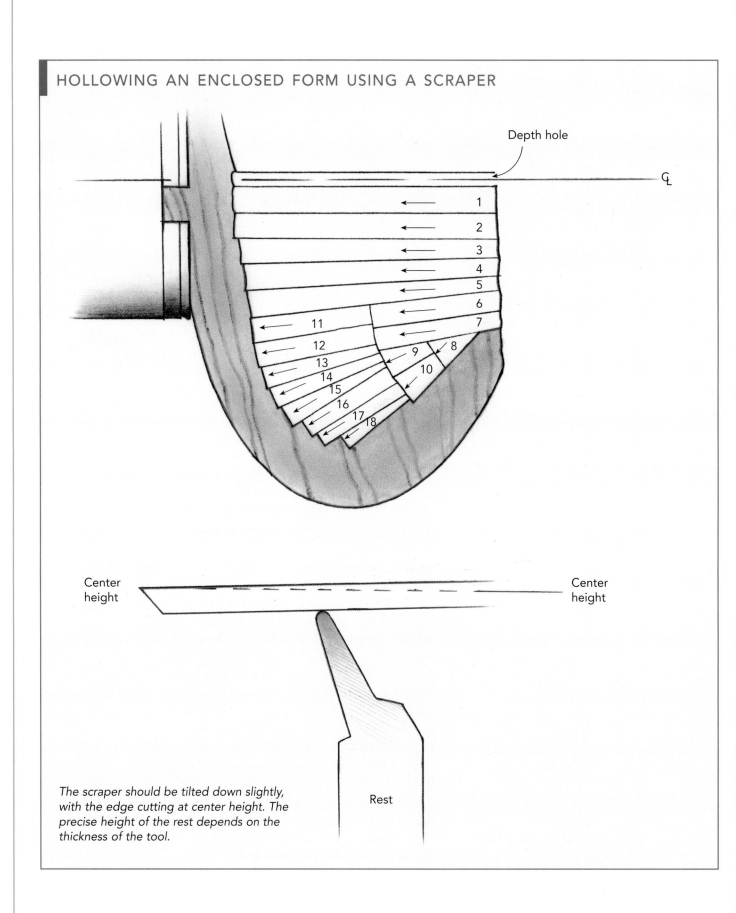

Depth hole

C̵L

Center height

Center height

Rest

The scraper should be tilted down slightly, with the edge cutting at center height. The precise height of the rest depends on the thickness of the tool.

Remember to let the wood come to the tool rather than forcing it. This means that as you approach center, where the wood is moving more slowly, you need to slow the rate at which you move the tool forward. Pushing too hard, trying to cut too big a shaving, can lead to a catch.

Letting the tool come to the wood is especially important when cutting intermittently, as in the upper parts of a natural-edge bowl (see the photo on p. 93). In this situation it's important to decide the line you are going to cut and take the tool along that line regardless of whether there is wood to cut or not. Any pressure against the wood will push the edge into the gap, risking a catch.

Another source of catches is failing to continue the cut all the way to center; it allows a shoulder to develop, which is easy to forget as you enjoy the shavings. If the right wing of the edge contacts the shoulder, the leverage on the edge is instantly magnified, and if you're not prepared for it, it can lever the tool out of your hand. If you're gripping the tool hard, more likely the bowl will fly from the chuck. Try not to let a shoulder build up, but if it does, treat it like the rim of the bowl and make a series of entry cuts until the curve flows from rim to center.

Continue hollowing until the wall is about one-tenth the diameter of the bowl.

HOLLOWING WITH SCRAPERS

I rarely encourage the use of scrapers for rough-hollowing, partly because in most situations they are much less efficient than a gouge for bulk removal of waste, but mostly because they are best kept for the final finishing cuts. On natural-edge bowls, small gouges will cut the undulating rim more cleanly than a scraper, although scrapers are useful in the lower, solid sections. Scrapers are excellent for hollowing enclosed forms since they're easier to control than a gouge, especially in the upper portions of an enclosed form (see the top illustration on

To absorb any small catches, get your weight over the tool with the handle aligned under your forearm and against your side.

the facing page). When hollowing with a scraper, have the tool aligned under your forearm and against your side to absorb any catches.

A scraper demands a finer sense of touch than a gouge; it's easy to push the edge too forcefully against the wood and have a catch. Never use more than one-quarter of the edge at a time because the pressure of the wood against an edge that large is difficult to control, especially cutting well over the rest, when leverage increases.

You can remove waste fastest using a ¾-in. to 1-in. (19mm to 25mm) square-end scraper working in a series of steps (see the top illustration on the facing page). Working within the diameter of the chuck (cuts 1 through 5), you can be quite forceful, pushing the edge into the wood with the force parallel to the lathe axis and using up to ½ in. (13mm) of the edge. Keep the tool tilted down slightly, with the edge cutting at about center height, as shown in the bottom illustration on the facing page. Catches most likely occur at the end of a cut when the right side of the edge suddenly contacts the wood, greatly increasing the pressure on the edge and consequently the leverage you have to control. To avoid this, stop each cut slightly short of the previous cut—something you'll usually need to do anyway because bowls are rarely flat inside. Then a final cut can sweep across the bottom curve to flatten out the steps, although when roughing bowls I normally don't waste the time.

Scrapers are more useful once you start undercutting the rim (cuts 8 through 10) when the handle lies at a far more convenient angle than that of a gouge. I continue to use a square-end scraper to remove most of the waste, then remove the steps with a round-nose scraper.

The scraper must be kept flat on the rest for this cut or the raised side is liable to be snapped down onto the rest. Few of us have the strength to control even a small catch when holding the end of a handle so, as with most tools, I have my right hand near the ferrule and the handle aligned under my forearm as shown in the photo on p. 95. My left hand ensures that the tool blade stays flat on the rest while deflecting the shavings.

Saving the Center: Bowl-Coring Techniques

Up until the 20th century, bowls were made on pole lathes whose reciprocating action enabled nests of bowls to be turned from a single block because the to-and-fro rotation of the lathe cleared the shavings from the hooked tools then in use. However, these techniques lapsed into obscurity with the introduction of continuously rotating powered lathes. A few bowl manufacturers invested in coring systems, but most turners didn't bother because the wood was cheap. Only when timber prices rose dramatically in the mid 1970s and bowl turning became a popular hobby and source of income for a whole new generation of woodturners was serious attention once again applied to coring out and saving the inside of bowls.

These days rough-turning and nesting bowls in green wood is again standard practice for professional bowl turners. Turning the center of a blank into several bowls greatly increases the

With practice and very stable wood, it's possible to save at least two more bowls from within a bowl this size.

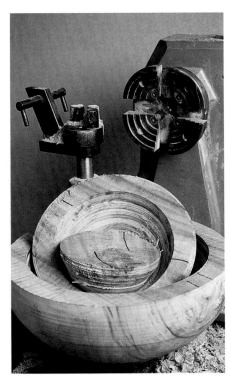

*Rough-turning and nesting bowls in green wood
is again standard practice for professional bowl turners.*

profit margin. Not having to wait years for heavy-section lumber to air-dry and avoiding the tedious task of always working dry wood is also an attraction.

Rough bowls are cut from the inside only after the profile has been established. There are two broad approaches to saving a bowl center: working from the right (or tailstock side) and working from the left (or headstock side). Most coring devices are set up so you work from the right on a bowl gripped by the foot (see the photos on the facing page) and you remove bowls, smallest first, from the center outwards. Alternatively you can work from the left as shown in the photos at right and peel bowls, larger to smaller, from the core. Whichever side you work from, the techniques are much the same, though each approach has its advantages and disadvantages.

I prefer to nest bowls from the left for two reasons. First, the blank is held securely by a screw or screws that grip the blank through layers of fibers. When you work from the right, the bowl is much less securely gripped by a chuck; the grain in the foot can easily split if you apply too much force to the outer portions of the bowl.

Second, and of more relevance to a production turner, as one bowl is peeled off the blank, the core is still there ready for the operation to be repeated. This makes the process much faster than from the right, where each portion of the center saved needs to be rechucked. The fact that the blank is so securely held when working from the left means that considerably more force can be applied to the cut, which in turn speeds the process. The downside of nesting from the left is that the headstock prevents

Keep the handle into your side to gain maximum support for the tool, your left arm bearing against the front of the lathe.

Slicing from the left to release a nested bowl. Note that the core from which you can slice another bowl remains mounted in position.

Salad Bowls

The smaller bowl was saved from within the larger using the Stewart System Slicer. The roughed bowls were seasoned for about a year before being completed.

MATERIAL:	Claret ash
SIZES:	14½ in. by 6⅝ in. (370mm by 170mm), 11¾ in. by 4 in. (300mm by 100mm)

the use of small-radius cutters. But there is no problem using a straight slicer, except that all the blanks saved are for outflowing bowls. That's a small price to pay for the speed and efficiency.

In the late 1970s, a number of experimental coring devices were thrust into the market, most of which have vanished. Today there are several systems commercially available offering curved and straight cutters that enable you to extract at least three bowls from a typical bowl blank. Of these, the following two are almost universally recommended.

THE STEWART SYSTEM SLICER

One of the earliest and still one of the best bowl-coring systems is the Stewart System Slicer. The Slicer is a round bar tapering to a narrow but deep end with a carbide tip similar to those on a circular saw blade. The kerf is relatively narrow and the tool is used with a standard rest. A pistol-grip handle increases your leverage. There's an optional longer handle with an arm brace for very deep cuts, but I rarely find the need to use it. The disadvantage of the Slicer is that it cuts only in a straight line, which means that all the saved bowls will be outflowing like those shown in the photo at left. But against that, it's handy for saving rings of wood from very large blanks and from the lower half of wide-rimmed bowls, as shown in the photos on the facing page. Being thin, it cuts very fast.

To save a ring, you make two cuts: first from the bottom, then from the side, each angled toward the other. You use the Slicer horizontally with the tip cutting at center height, and you need to make at least two cuts to give the thickening blade entry into the wood for deeper cuts.

I err on the side of caution when pushing the tool in, so as not to go any deeper than I need to. I try to make the final cut from the bottom, separating the ring from the base (rather than from the side) so that I can catch it on the tool. If the ring is separated from the side, it can easily spin off and race around the floor in a possibly dangerous manner.

From larger rings like the one shown front left in the bottom photo at right on the facing page, you can cut a number of small bowls, the sale of which will more than pay for the original blank. Once seasoned, rings can also be used for picture and mirror frames or even to enlarge a smaller bowl glued in place as a wide rim.

The Slicer is used in exactly the same way to separate bowls during the nesting process. In the top photo on p. 97, I'm using the tool from the left. Note that the handle is against my torso for maximum control against the tool snatching and that my left arm is tucked against the headstock. Aim the cut at a point just above the center of the bowl base.

Because the tool shank is wider than the tip, the deeper you cut, the wider the opening of the cut needs to be to accommodate the thicker portion of the Slicer blade. To broaden the opening, you'll need two or three cuts as shown in the illustration on p. 100. A face shield is essential for this operation because the Slicer flings out sizable curved and razor-edged chunks at high speeds to bounce around the

Rings saved from very large blanks or wide-rimmed bowls can be cut into small blanks or glued to small bowls to increase their diameter. The 20-in. (501mm) she-oak ring shown here yielded 10 small bowls, each 4⅝ in. (120mm) diameter and 2⅜ in. (60mm) high.

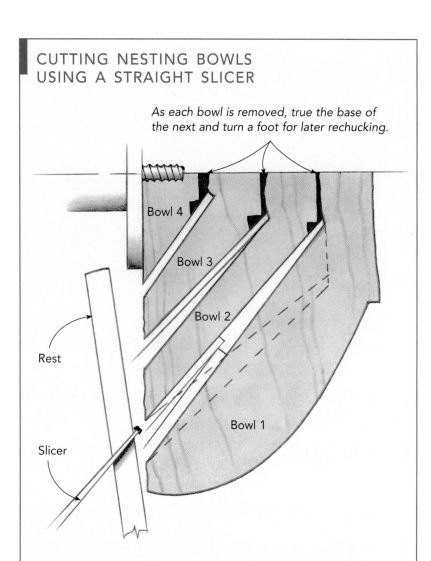

CUTTING NESTING BOWLS USING A STRAIGHT SLICER

As each bowl is removed, true the base of the next and turn a foot for later rechucking.

Bowl 4

Bowl 3

Bowl 2

Bowl 1

Rest

Slicer

The bowl outlines are what you should save, but it is worth making the initial cuts along the dotted lines to give the tool more room. If it doesn't, widen the bottom of the opening until the outer bowl can be split away.

For the frequent occasions when the central bowl or a cone becomes jammed on a screw chuck, I have a pipe wrench ready to go. A standard C-wrench (black handle visible) keeps the chuck from unwinding as pressure is applied.

workshop. Any spectators within range should also have face protection, although the process is best done with nobody close by.

As shavings and dust build up within the kerf, the tool can jam, bringing the operation to a sudden halt. Two things happen simultaneously: The tool kicks up as it twists and jams in the curved opening, and the lathe stops, the belt slipping and screaming. The sooner you hit

the off button the better. In this situation you want a lathe to stop instantly, and some electronic braking systems prevent this. Check that your lathe is set up so it will stop rotating the moment you hit the off switch.

It is difficult to see what is happening as cutting proceeds, but as the connecting portion narrows, the bowl will begin to wobble somewhat, warning that it is about to come off. At this point, stop the lathe and give the bowl a sharp blow with the heel of your hand or pry it free gently using a small crowbar. It should break free easily, as the wood splits along the grain (see the bottom photo on p. 97). If not, cut a little further.

The main advantage of the McNaughton system
over a straight slicer is that it cuts curves.

Once the bowl is removed, use a shallow gouge to create a foot on the remaining cone and smooth the profile before repeating the process to extract a smaller bowl. Frequently the final small bowl or cone will be very difficult to remove from a screw chuck by hand, so I always have a pipe wrench close by. In this situation, locking the spindle is rarely sufficient, and you must prevent the chuck from unwinding by using a long bar or wrench as shown in the photo on the facing page. Often the foot needs lengthening to provide enough purchase for the wrench jaws.

THE McNAUGHTON BOWL SAVER

Of the later bowl-nesting systems, the McNaughton is generally acknowledged as the one to choose and use. The McNaughton system uses a curved blade, a vertical gate to keep the tool upright as it moves into the wood, and an antikick bar to prevent the edge from being dragged down. Cutters, as shown in the top photo at right, are available for working from both the left (headstock side) and right (tailstock side).

The gate is set up on the tool rest support with the cutting edge at center height. Having established the correct height of the cutter edge by aligning it with a center as shown in the photo at right, I cut a line into the tool post so I can now set the gate assembly quickly and easily by eye. Alternatively, have a locking collar on the shaft, or a pin through it to allow you to locate the gate accurately without even looking.

The main advantage of the McNaughton system over a straight slicer is that it cuts curves and can cut right to center. In addition, the

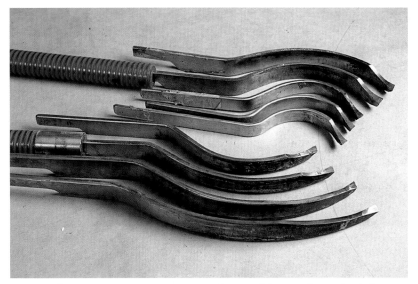

McNaughton system cutters are manufactured for use from the left (lower group) or the right (upper group).

Set the McNaughton system gate so the cutters are at center height. A sawn line marks the height on the tool post so that the gate height can be relocated quickly and easily by eye.

On large, unbalanced blanks, use a tail center for security.

The saved center of a bowl needs a foot for rechucking, and this is most easily turned when the blank is jammed against the bowl from which it's just come.

blades are sufficiently inexpensive that if a severe catch bends a blade, purchasing a replacement is no big deal. A large cutter pays for itself in two or three saved bowls.

The minor drawbacks are the width of the cutting edge, which can make cutting a lot slower, and its lack of a carbide tip. You keep the edge sharp by honing and very occasional grinding. When working from the left side, the headstock prevents the use of the smaller blades, whereas on the right, no such problem prevails if the tail center is removed. Consequently, since most people work on a smaller scale, the right-side cutters are more readily available than the left, which might need to be ordered.

In the photos on p. 96, you can see that the inner bowl broke free before the cutter reached

center. With practice and very stable wood, it's possible to save at least two more bowls from within a bowl this size.

As the cut proceeds, wiggle the handle slightly so the kerf is a little wider than the cutting edge. This helps the shavings to escape, but it's still a good idea to withdraw the tool frequently to prevent a buildup of dust and chips that can jam the tool.

When the slicer is reluctant to go in, try adjusting the position of the rest slightly. With practice you can do this with the lathe running, adjusting the rest as you push the tool in and locking it in position as the cut becomes easier. When I do this, my knee is ever by the off bar, in case things go wrong.

Working from the left, you can use only the large-radius cutters.

When coring large, unbalanced blanks, as shown in the photo at left on the facing page, I prefer to use tail-center support for safety.

Blanks saved from the bowl centers when working from the right need rechucking, either on the original screw fixing or reversed and held between the bowl from which they've just come and the tail center, as shown in the photo at right on the facing page. Once remounted, turn a foot on the base so that it can be gripped for hollowing.

When using the McNaughton system from the left as shown in the photo above, there are no such problems because you turn a foot on the cone that remains after the outer bowl is peeled away. When working from the left, I have two rests in action—one next to the head-stock with the gate assembly set in position, the other toward the tailstock with a T-rest ready to go for putting a foot on each of the inner cones as it is revealed.

The McNaughton system requires practice (like most activities). Aligning the curved slicer so you don't cut too deeply and go through the bottom of the bowl can be tricky. Sound will tell you a lot, but sadly you have to learn this for yourself or watch an expert using the tool and listen. Although the cutter is wider than the blade, the shavings still tend to build up, which in turn can jam the bowl to a halt. If you are pushing the tool forward and nothing seems to be happening, chances are there are shavings jammed on the edge. Stop the lathe and clear the shavings.

Natural-edge blanks are cored using exactly the same techniques, although the McNaughton system is easier to use on uneven surfaces because its slicer is held in the gate.

For internal finishing cuts, see chapter 7.

6 COMPLETING THE PROFILE

To complete a profile, you want to have the rough-turned bowl or (if you're not rough-turning) the blank mounted so you can work all the way around it without the tail center getting in the way. Solid blanks will be on a screw chuck or faceplate, so there's no problem with access. The most straightforward way to grip a roughed bowl securely so you can complete the profile is to mount it over a chuck.

During the months or even years that rough-turned bowls lie seasoning, they will warp, which makes them difficult to remount on the lathe securely. So before looking at the gouge and scraping techniques that produce fine surfaces off the tool (reducing sanding to a minimum), let's consider how you can remount warped bowls and salvage bowls from seemingly impossible situations.

Remounting Roughed-Out Bowls

If you are using screws and a faceplate, flatten the base on a belt sander or using a handplane before fixing the bowl. Never pass a bowl across a planer. Take careful note of exactly how far the screws project from the faceplate so you know how far they'll penetrate the wood; you don't want to run into them when hollowing. If you aligned the screws along the grain when fixing the bowl for roughing, the screws should relocate in the original holes.

If your original screw holes were across the grain, chances are they will have moved closer and no longer align with the holes in your faceplate. You'll need to make additional screw holes, and you can end up with a messy base with holes off center, unless you place the new screw holes midway between the old, as shown in the illustration on the facing page. First, rule a line A through the old holes and draw another line B at 90 degrees midway between the two. Set your screws on line B, so that eventually you'll be filling four holes evenly balanced about center.

In the days when I used a three-jaw engineer's chuck to hold just about every job on the lathe, roughing out a bowl included turning a shoulder on the inside, against which to expand the chuck jaws later for finish-turning. Grabbing a warped surface is never a problem with three jaws. But the chucks are slow to operate and the jaws dangerous, which is why the self-centering four-jaw chucks are now universally favored. However, in order to provide a secure fixing, four-jaw chucks do need a true surface against which to expand or contract. So the first task in remounting a seasoned rough-turned bowl is to turn a shoulder on the inside of the bowl for the chuck to grip. Holding a severely warped bowl so you can turn enough of a shoulder can involve chucking and rechucking several times.

The basic routine is to grip the roughed bowl by its foot as shown in the top left photo on p. 106. Then, using a ⅜-in. (9mm) deep-fluted gouge, true the rim and also the upper quarter to third of the inside, creating a shoulder for the chuck to grip. I begin with the gouge rolled over about 45 degrees, easing the left wing of the tool into the uneven rim until the tick-tick noise stops, indicating a trued surface (see the top right photo on p. 106). Then I bring the bevel to rub on the trued surface and cut toward center as shown in the bottom left photo on p. 106. (This process of truing the rim must be repeated before finish-hollowing; see pp. 130-131).

Finally, I use a square-end scraper to create the chucking shoulder (see the bottom right photo on p. 106). The wider the diameter the chuck grips the better, but in case I put in too wide a shoulder for my chuck, as did happen here, I'll put in one smaller as insurance. It is important to have trimmed the rim as part of this process. When you remount the bowl, a trued rim confirms instantly that the bowl is seated accurately. It also establishes the overall dimensions with which you'll be working as you complete the profile.

For remounting natural-edge bowls, make the shoulder long enough so if you need to realign the rim, you can adjust the bowl over the chuck.

LOCATING A FACEPLATE ON AN OVAL BASE

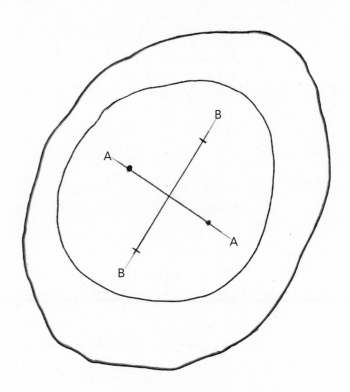

When the original screw holes in a seasoned bowl have shrunk closer, it looks better if the new screws are aligned between the old. First, rule a line (A) through the old holes, then draw another line (B) at 90 degrees midway between the two. Set your new faceplate screws on line B the same distance from center as the old holes, so that eventually you'll be filling four holes evenly balanced about center.

When expanding the chuck jaws into the shoulder as shown in the photo at right on p. 107, tighten the jaws firmly by hand as you might a water tap. Enough is enough; you don't need to exert pressure that can split a bowl. If you hear any unusual cracking noises as you tighten the chuck, inspect the surface of the bowl closely for developing splits. On some older chucks where the collar is a bit loose, it is possible that the jaws will expand slightly with

To prepare a bowl for expanding jaws, grip the roughed bowl by the foot, then true the rim. Next, true the upper portion of the inside and form a squared shoulder against which the jaws can expand.

To assess how thick a bowl wall might be when trued, scribe pencil lines on the rim. Here I've partly trued the inside and marked the point on the outer lip of the rim nearest center. At the bottom between the original rough-turned surface and the line, you can see there is plenty of wood available.

If the bowl fits right over the chuck, you might not be able to use the tommy bar or key provided with most chucks. For this lever-operated chuck, I use an Allen key as an angled bar, although typically in this situation I use the C-wrench on top of the headstock along with the standard tommy bar.

centrifugal force when you switch on the lathe. If this happens, you will hear a slight crack—a noise like a remote whip crack or pistol shot. Again, anything unusual like this must be investigated to find the cause before proceeding.

All this seems simple enough, but often the foot will have warped in such a way that it won't fit into the chuck or causes the bowl to rotate well off center. Mostly the foot distorts to an oval so that only four of the eight corners of the chuck jaws can contact the wood. Center the bowl in the chuck as well as you can by eye. Then, to ascertain whether or not there's a bowl still within the roughed form, mark on the rim with pencil the widest point of the inside and the narrowest point of the outside as I am doing in the photo at left above. If there is enough of a

foot to grip, you can adjust the alignment of the bowl in the chuck for a thicker bowl wall, then, provided the bowl is secure in the chuck, you can turn a small shoulder against which the chuck can expand. In this situation, the bowl might not be as securely held as you'd like, so be very cautious as you turn the shoulder.

Sometimes a roughed bowl warps so much that there seems no prospect of turning it true. These are best mounted between centers as shown in the photo on p. 108, with the tail center pressing the bowl over a large improvised drive, such as a big faceplate, a chuck with the jaws wide open, or an MDF disc on a screw chuck. Hold the bowl over the driving component (here an MDF disc) and adjust the form by eye before bringing in tail-center support. The bowl can be aligned by eye in relation to the rest or using pencil lines, much as with the natural-edge bowl shown in the bottom left and center photos on p. 70. When the alignment is about right, tighten the tail center so the bowl is pressed firmly against the drive, turn a foot, and

Severely or asymmetrically warped bowls are best centered over a large drive and tail-center support. The drive is an MDF disc with a chamfered edge that fits into the bowl.

true the profile. Often the bowl will slip out of alignment; therefore, get the foot done first so that you have something to grip.

Don't forget to turn the base flat or slightly concave so it seats in the chuck. Work right into the center using a shallow gouge, leaving a nub about ½ in. (13mm) in diameter to support the tail center. This nub can be removed later. If the bowl is barely secure between centers, the moment you have enough of a foot to grip, remount the bowl into a chuck and proceed to true the rim and cut an internal shoulder as shown in the photos on p. 106.

If the bowl is absolutely secure between centers, you might as well complete the profile as much as possible now using the gouge and scraper techniques discussed in "Completing the Profile" on pp. 116-121 and "Scrapers and Shear-Scraping" on pp. 121-125. The stub at center can easily be removed off the lathe and the rough area finished by hand. This is a good way to mount large bowls that you cannot grip satisfactorily from the inside with your chuck. Then your problem becomes how to hold this for hollowing; options are offered in chapter 7.

Mounting between a driving disc and tail center is also a good option for fixing a very deep roughed bowl when the bowl fits so far over the chuck that the rim hits the headstock. One portion of a warped rim can be chiseled or planed away so the bowl rotates freely, but often this is not enough and you need an alternative chucking method.

You can also complete the profile with the bowl held by the foot, either in a chuck or more commonly on a faceplate or screw chuck. The latter remains a popular production method, but it does leave a hole to be plugged at center and often a base that is thicker than desirable aesthetically.

How you go about completing the profile depends in part on how you have fixed the bowl on the lathe. As you will see, a bowl mounted with the whole of the outside exposed enables you to use a broader range of cuts than one held by the base. Otherwise, the cuts used with either method of fixing mirror each other.

Truing the Profile

When the roughed bowl is remounted on the lathe with the profile fully exposed, it needs to be turned true before you do anything else (see the photo at left on the facing page). Then you know exactly how much material you have to play with. True the profile with refined versions of the gouge cuts you used to rough the profile originally. The idea is to skim away the eccentricity, removing only what is necessary to make the form round. If you want to turn any more away, ensure that the bowl wall is thick enough.

If one area sounds hollow or like a drum,
that's probably because it's thin.

True the profile with a series of arcing cuts, beginning in sections where the eccentricity is greatest in order to reduce any vibration as soon as possible.

It's easy to forget that you are not working a solid block of wood at this stage.

The bowl wall will likely be much thinner in some areas than others, so pay attention to the sounds. If one area sounds hollow or like a drum, that's probably because it's thin. One advantage of having a newly turned shoulder for the jaws to grip is that you can take the bowl on and off the chuck to check wall thickness and be reasonably sure that it will go back on accurately.

There are no such problems if the bowl is held by the base, but you need a slightly different set of tools and techniques than for those

with the bowl mounted the other way around. You will need a steep bevel on your gouge, as shown in the top photo on p. 110, and a scraper skewed to the right, seen in the bottom right photo on p. 122. Even then it is difficult to get a thrusting shear cut working in this situation, so you need to use pulling cuts similar to those shown in the photo above, unless working some burls where the grain is wild enough that cutting downhill (which would normally be against the grain) is not a problem. Working near the chuck can be awkward, raising stress levels if you're not used to it. But if you do run

To make shear cuts from the left, you'll need a steep bevel to enable you to start the cut as close as possible to the bottom, or cut against the grain as shown in the photo below left.

the cutting edge into the chuck, not to worry. That's why grinders were invented.

I don't like working left-handed (turning is quite difficult enough without trying to be ambidextrous), so I use pulling shear cuts to work away from the chuck jaws as shown in the photo at right on p. 109. In the lower portions of the profile where a conventional shear cut is difficult, it's always worth trying a cut against the grain toward the base (see the photo at left below) or toward the rim on an enclosed form with a raised detail at the rim (see the photo at right below). As you cut against the grain in either direction, you stand square to the bowl, so you can watch the form developing on the upper horizon of the bowl. If you go steadily

When truing a profile held by the base in a chuck, as above, you have to cut against the grain near the chuck jaws. If you want some raised detail at the rim of an enclosed bowl, as at right, the curve is easier to cut working against the grain here, too. By not forcing the tool into the wood, you should obtain a surface ready for sanding.

and don't force the edge into the wood, you'll probably cut a surface clean enough for sanding. On burl you can usually cut in either direction and get a good result.

If you have any beads blocked out (as shown in the bottom right photo on the facing page), they should be trued along with everything else. When turning a detail on the outer lip of a rim, first cut from the rim, then cut the shoulder (see the top photo at right). In each case the gouge is pointing in the direction you're cutting.

Now is also the time to assess any features you might not want, such as splits or knots, and to decide what you're going to do about them. Small knots and splits can be filled with dust and cyanoacrylate (Super Glue) adhesive (see the bottom photo at right). Get rid of everything you don't want in your final bowl now rather than risk discovering the remnants of the rough-turned surface when the bowl is almost completed and they're difficult to get rid of.

All parts of a rough bowl should be trued, including blocked-out beads.

Final Decisions Concerning the Profile

Once the profile is round again, it is time for the final shaping and deciding on how you will hold the bowl for finish-hollowing. Most of the bowls I make have a foot, which means that at this stage I can complete the profile while ensuring that the foot fits one of my chucks. It's been a good way to go for production: I can turn a foot from 1 in. to 8 in. (25mm to 200mm) in diameter, knowing that with a minor adjustment I can fit it to a set of jaws. This allows me to establish the overall dimensions of the bowl knowing that at worst I'll need to reduce the diameter of the foot slightly. And by having the chuck contract around the foot, I gain maximum support for the bowl as I complete the hollowing.

To fill a knot, rub powdery dust into the split, then drip thin cyanoacrylate (super) glue into the area. The resin will percolate the dust instantly and set within seconds, allowing work to continue with minimal delay.

These small cocobolo bowls were gripped around the grooves at the foot for hollowing, where the diameter is 2 in. (50mm).

Most expanding collets can function in a groove, so retain the central mass for decoration and to maintain weight and balance in the base.

The alternative chucking method for completing the profile is to expand the jaws within a recess in the base. This offers less support during hollowing but is a common enough practice, allowing you to have any shape you want in the lower portions of the bowl. Use the chuck jaws expanded as wide as possible for maximum support, but ensure that you have a good amount of material at the rim of the foot to withstand the pressure of the jaws. Even on small bowls, such as the example in the photo at left, I recommend a supporting rim of at least ½ in. (15mm), especially on wood known to split easily, such as oak, yew, or ash.

If I want a bowl with a rounded base, I leave a shoulder for the chuck to grip so I can hollow the bowl. I project the lower portion of the curve through the shoulder, which I turn away later, when gripping the bowl by the rim. Techniques for this approach are given on pp. 148–149.

Another favorite chucking technique for small outflowing bowls such as those shown in the photo above is to have long-nose jaws close around a groove.

I rarely have a chuck expanding within the base because the depth of wood required for the chuck recess and the diameter required to accommodate the pressure of the expanding jaws almost always compromise the design. It makes for a thicker and wider base than I generally consider desirable, particularly on smaller bowls.

Completing the Base

Before you complete the bowl profile, establish the diameter of the foot and complete the base. The underside needs to be slightly concave so that the bowl sits on the rim of the base. Turn the base using a small gouge as shown in the top photo at right. If the surface needs improving, try a skewed scraper as shown in the bottom photo at right. Initially have the scraper flat on the rest and use only a small portion of the edge at one time, stroking the surface with delicate sweeping cuts, moving the edge parallel to, rather than directly against, the surface. A smooth bottom can look somewhat bland, so if the bowl is footed, I usually add some decoration—like a groove or two (see p. 169).

If your chuck can grab the size foot you want, mark the diameter on the base (see the photos on p. 114) and turn a slightly oversize foot using a ⅜-in. (9mm) shallow fingernail gouge as shown in the photo on p. 115. As usual when beginning a cut in space, have the handle below horizontal, align the bevel in the direction you are cutting, and pivot the edge down into the wood by raising the handle. For the most secure grip, you want to create a slightly dovetailed foot. But you don't complete the foot or dovetail it at this stage in case it needs thinning or lowering, which would then reduce its diameter (see the illustration on p. 114).

The base should be turned slightly concave so it sits firmly on the rim. Use a small, shallow ⅜-in. (9mm) gouge with the bevel aligned in the direction you're cutting, or try a skewed scraper if the surface could be better.

For the most secure grip, you want to create a slightly dovetailed foot.

CHANGING DOVETAIL DIAMETERS

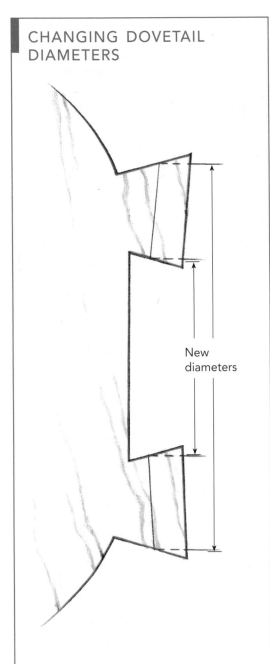

New diameters

A dovetailed foot, as well as a dovetailed recess in a foot, changes size if the foot is reduced in height, modifying the chucking diameter.

To adjust dividers to a chuck's diameter, fix one point on the rim of the chuck with a finger and adjust the other point to the maximum diameter (top). To transfer the diameter to the bowl base, mark the wood with the left point so the scribed circle aligns with the right point. The center (highlighted with a black dot) should lie midway between the two points. If the right point fails to line up with the circle, move the left point over half the distance between the right point and the circle (above).

Cut a foot using a small, shallow gouge. Start with the tool on its side, and align the bevel in the direction you are cutting.

When the profile is all but completed and ready for sanding, you'll come back to turn the foot to size. Ensure that it is the same diameter or smaller than the true diameter of the chuck jaws; otherwise the eight corners of the jaws will damage the wood. If the foot is slightly smaller than the jaw's diameter, the center of each jaw bears on the wood, as shown in the illustration at right, bruising it slightly but leaving a barely discernable mark.

If you are making a dovetailed recess for expanding jaws, make the base concave before turning the recess. If you make the dovetailed recess first, the recess will widen when you turn the base concave, which can be a problem if you are at the limits of the chuck (see the illustration on the facing page).

Most modern chucks need only a dovetailed groove in which to operate, and this is best turned using a small dovetail scraper (see the bottom photo on p. 112). You can purchase these, but they are easy to make yourself on a standard grinder from an old ½-in. (13mm)

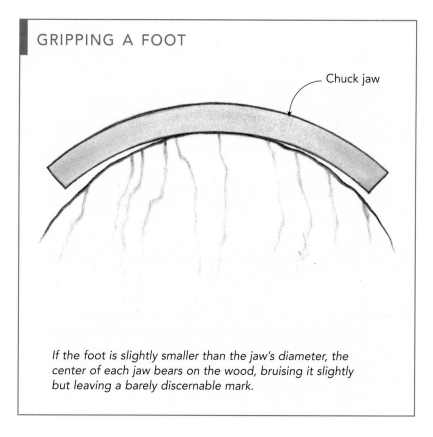

GRIPPING A FOOT

Chuck jaw

If the foot is slightly smaller than the jaw's diameter, the center of each jaw bears on the wood, bruising it slightly but leaving a barely discernable mark.

CHUCK RECESSES

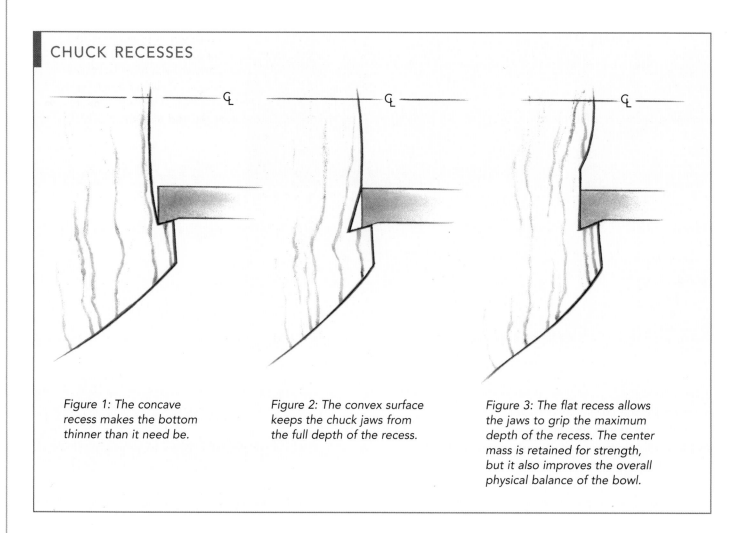

Figure 1: The concave recess makes the bottom thinner than it need be.

Figure 2: The convex surface keeps the chuck jaws from the full depth of the recess.

Figure 3: The flat recess allows the jaws to grip the maximum depth of the recess. The center mass is retained for strength, but it also improves the overall physical balance of the bowl.

square-section scraper or skew chisel. The groove must be flat; otherwise the chuck cannot grip properly and offer maximum support for the job as hollowing proceeds.

The illustration above shows three variations on the shape of the groove for chucking. In Figure 1, the concave recess makes the bottom thinner than it need be. In Figure 2, the convex surface keeps the chuck jaws from the full depth of the recess. In Figure 3, the flat recess allows the jaws to grip the maximum depth of the recess. The center mass is retained for strength, but it also improves the overall physical balance of the bowl. It looks better beaded, but to learn how to do that, see p. 169.

Completing the Profile

The approach here is to cut the curves as smoothly as possible using gouges, then clean up any undulations or torn end grain using scrapers. This is relatively easy when the bowl is mounted over a chuck and the whole of the outside is exposed.

Remember to cut from smaller to larger diameter, so that each fiber you cut is supported by another (until you get to the rim or fullness of the curve). If your profile has a foot, you will be unable to start the cut at the bottom of the curve, so start as close to the foot as possible. For the section just above the foot, where you have to cut against the grain, use a shallow

To cut into a foot against the grain, go very gently but firmly using a ⅜-in. (9mm) shallow gouge. To avoid a catch, make sure that the gouge is on its side at the end of the cut.

gouge with a long fingernail grind. My favorite tool in this situation, as for most detailing, is a ⅜-in. (9mm) shallow gouge seen in the photo above. Cutting the curve is directly against unsupported end grain, so you need to go very gently. When cutting into the corner, either from the curve or the foot, it is essential to roll the tool right on its side at the end of the cut to avoid a catch.

The easiest way to cut flowing curves is to have the gouge pointing in the direction you are cutting so you can steer it where you want to go, as shown in the photo at right. As always, the cleanest cut is obtained when the edge lies at about 45 degrees to the oncoming wood. To achieve this, hold a shallow gouge rolled over about 45 degrees with the bevel rubbing the wood so that the upper side of the nose of the tool is at the best angle (see the photo at left on p. 118). Better still, use the right wing of a heavier deep-fluted gouge, flute up, as shown in the photo at right on p. 118, for what is known as a

An underhand grip, with your forefinger hooked under the rest, enables you to pull the tool firmly onto the rest. As the cut proceeds around the curve, you'll need to stop to adjust your grip around the rest. This deep-fluted gouge can be used flute up for a "back cut."

The cleanest cut occurs when the portion of the edge cutting lies at about 45 degrees to the oncoming wood. To achieve this, use a shallow gouge rolled over about 45 degrees and rub the bevel (above). Or use a deep-fluted gouge, flute up (right). Notice that despite the different tool positions, the relationship between edge and wood is the same.

"back cut." This cut can be done only with the deep-fluted tool, which has the vertical side bevel to support the edge. If you try to use the side of a shallow tool where there's no bevel to rub, the tool will catch every time.

I like to have my right hand on the ferrule with the handle tucked against my forearm so the tool is like an extension to my arm, as shown in the photo on the facing page. (I apply a similar strategy when hollowing, as shown in the top left photo on p. 91). To cut smooth curves, you will need to move smoothly with the tool, cutting in a series of arcs. If you can keep your weight behind the tool and your movements smooth and flowing, smooth and flowing curves should follow. You must decide the trajectory of your cut and take the tool on that line (see the illustration on the facing

page). If the trajectory of the cut seems to be heading into space (A), just follow that line. Then bring the tool back and start again well down the curve with a progressively deeper cut. If you move the handle suddenly, you change the direction you're cutting and create a soft angle. Smooth curves require a series of smooth movements.

If you sense that you are cutting too deep (B), stop immediately and assess the situation because you'll probably have to change either your bowl foot or the overall curve of the profile. Remember, too, to check available wall thickness.

Often the tool will start chattering about halfway up the profile—you'll hear a knocking sound, but the three or four very broad chatter marks that result are often difficult to discern. When this happens, begin the cut again lower down the curve and keep the tool tight to the

DEVELOPING CURVES

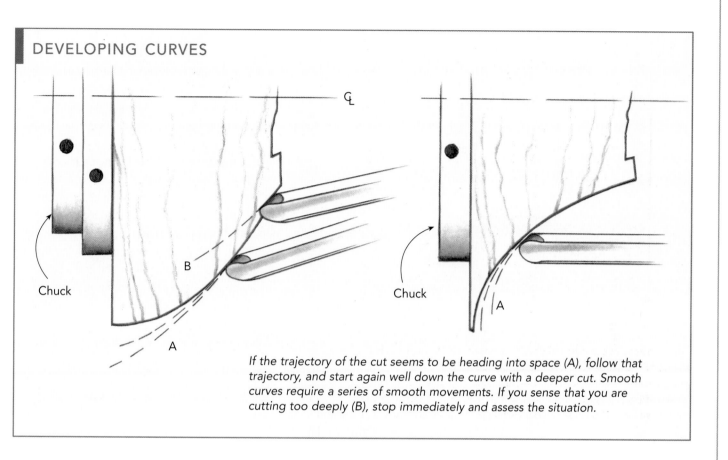

If the trajectory of the cut seems to be heading into space (A), follow that trajectory, and start again well down the curve with a deeper cut. Smooth curves require a series of smooth movements. If you sense that you are cutting too deeply (B), stop immediately and assess the situation.

rest, either pulling it down if you're using an underhand grip or leaning on it with an overhand grip.

Concave curves require a gouge with a steep right bevel and a softened bevel shoulder, which is less likely to mark the wood as it rubs. Soften the bevel shoulder with a fine hone or on a buffing wheel. If you attempt to use a long bevel on a concave curve, you'll have a problem keeping the bevel rubbing and the fulcrum near the point of cut (see the photo at right).

Convex curves are generally easier to cut using a long-beveled gouge because for most of the cut you can get behind the tool and push it forward with a minimum of body movement. Cutting a smooth curve with a steeper bevel is more difficult because of the angle of the tool and the position of the handle in relation to the

When cutting a curve, I like to have my right hand on the ferrule with the handle tucked against my forearm, so the tool is like an extension to my arm. To cut the upper portion of the curve, I change my grip on the rest to allow the tool to move more freely.

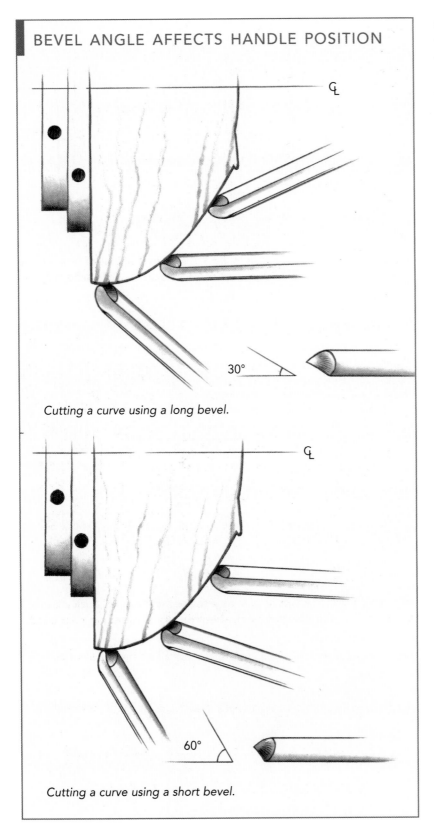

BEVEL ANGLE AFFECTS HANDLE POSITION

C̶L̶

30°

Cutting a curve using a long bevel.

C̶L̶

60°

Cutting a curve using a short bevel.

curve. The illustration at left demonstrates how the position of the tool handle depends on the tool's bevel angle as the bevel rides the profile.

To cut an enclosed form, you'll need to work from the rim back to the fullness of the curve as shown in the top photo at left on the facing page. The cuts are a mirror image of those you've just made from the base, the only problem being that the headstock can get in the way when working on smaller bowls. When the form curves into a narrow rim, you can use a gouge with a steeper bevel, but I usually sand and polish the lower portion of the form at this stage and complete the upper curve from the other direction when the bowl is remounted for hollowing (see the top photo at right on the facing page).

Cylindrical bowls and surfaces (like those shown in the photo at left on p. 80 and the photo on p. 136) demand the same cuts, tool-handling techniques, and attention to the basic rules.

To cut a natural edge with the bark still on, use the same approach as for the rest of the bowl profile. You need to decide the line the tool has to take and move it along that line regardless of what is or isn't there. The bevel contacts the wood but is not pushed against it. If the bark is staying on, it will likely prevent too much tearout of the fibers just below. However, you'll usually get a better surface off the tool by cutting in from the rim even if it is against the grain. Starting the cut can be tricky because at first there is so little profile to see or for the bevel to rub. If you look down the line of the profile from the rim, you should be able to work out the trajectory of your cut so it flows into the line already cut from the base. Any bumps where they meet are best eliminated by shear-scraping (see the next section).

Chatter marks are usually the result of pushing the tool too hard into the cut and against the wood. Try a lighter cut, keeping the tool firmly on the rest, then let the wood come to

To cut an enclosed form, you'll need to work from the rim back to the fullness of the curve.

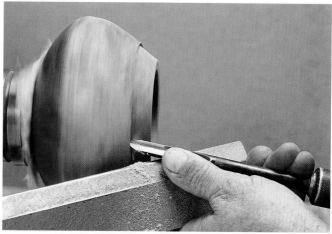

It is usually easier to work the upper sections of an enclosed bowl's profile once it has been rechucked for hollowing.

the tool, aiming to cut through the ridges and across the dips. If this doesn't work, try some delicate shear-scraping. When all else fails, there are always abrasives, which are dealt with in chapter 9.

Scrapers and Shear-Scraping

Scraping, and particularly shear-scraping, can significantly improve a gouge-cut surface. In part, this is because gouges leave a miniscule groove as they move across the surface they cut. A scraper held gently against the surface will remove the sides of the groove, often improving the surface. A scraper tilted on its side so the edge is presented to the wood at an angle will shear most wood clean. Another advantage of shear-scraping is that there is very little pressure against the wood so the edge is unlikely to catch unless working near corners.

I have three scrapers in constant use when completing the outside of a bowl. Each is designed for shear-scraping, with rounded sides for slipping along the roughest rest. I also use a ½-in. (13mm) gouge on its side as a scraper—the

A gouge can be used on its side as a scraper to clean up small areas; the technique can be convenient when the tool is already in your hand.

Working around a curve, you'll need to move the rest often to keep the fulcrum close to the point of cut.

Enclosed Form

Small enclosed bowls are ideal for potpourri, but many get used for strings of beads and similar jewelry. These forms also sit very nicely in the hand as personal nut and potato chip bowls.

MATERIAL:	Tasmanian myrtle
SIZE:	6 in. by 4 in. (150mm by 100mm)

The long point of a skewed scraper can reach into a corner without catching, provided you keep it flat on the rest.

bevel not rubbing—as shown in the bottom photo on p. 121, where there is no bead or other detail on which it might catch. The shallow gouge is easier to use because you can see what you're doing better than with a deep-fluted tool. In either case the curved edge is not as effective as the straighter scrapers, but it's a very handy way of cleaning up small areas when the tool is already in your hand.

To shear-scrape using a gouge, position the tool almost on its side with the flute facing the surface to be cut. Move the edge across the surface, brushing it in a series of sweeps, so the blade moves back and forth on the rest rather than across it toward the wood.

Skewed scrapers can be used flat or on edge. Used flat, the long point can reach into corners (see the photos above), but mostly you use the

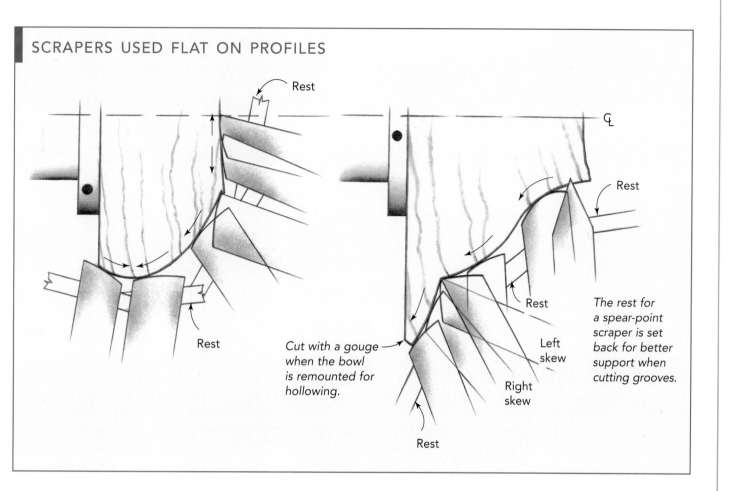

SCRAPERS USED FLAT ON PROFILES

Rest

Rest

C̵L

Rest

Rest

Cut with a gouge
when the bowl
is remounted for
hollowing.

Rest

Right
skew

Left
skew

*The rest for
a spear-point
scraper is set
back for better
support when
cutting grooves.*

center of the edge to take a shaving by pulling the tool along the rest so the edge just brushes the surface to cut very thin ribbons of shavings as shown in the photo at right and the illustration above. The pressure of the tool against the wood is similar to that of rubbing your hands together under a hot air dryer. When used flat, scrapers should be kept horizontal or pitched slightly down so that in the event of a catch the edge carries into space.

Almost the only time I move any scraper directly against and into the wood is when making the small decorative grooves on outflowing bowls whose primary purpose is to locate the chuck jaws when the bowl is gripped for hollowing, as shown in the top left photo on p. 124 (also see the top right photo on p. 129).

Use the center of a scraper's edge to take a shaving. Pull the tool along the rest so the edge just brushes the surface to cut very thin ribbons of shavings.

To cut small V-grooves cleanly, ease the spear-point scraper into the wood very gently.

To shear-scrape, tilt the scraper so the edge is presented at about 45 degrees to the oncoming wood.

A spear-point scraper enables you to shear-scrape right into corners.

To shear-scrape, tilt the scraper on its side so that the edge is presented at about 45 degrees to the oncoming wood, as shown in the top right photo on the facing page. The edge should exert very little pressure against the wood, and you have plenty of control over the leverage. The rotation of the bowl pulls the edge away from the work, so you can use any part of the edge without too much risk of a catch, although the lower half is preferable. Be sure to keep the scraper on the rest at all times. You cannot use the skewed scraper to shear-cut into the top of a foot or any detail because the underside of the bevel will catch.

Stroke the surface in a series of gentle pull cuts, working from smaller to larger diameter. Working around a curve, you'll need to move the rest often to keep the fulcrum close to the point of cut. On enclosed forms, you'll need to use a right-skewed scraper, as shown in the bottom right photo on p. 122 or a spear-point scraper. If you have only a left-skewed scraper, wait until the bowl is remounted for hollowing and complete the job then. This is my usual approach, and it has the advantage that I can true the rim at the same time since it is often a fraction out.

A spear-point scraper enables you to shear-scrape right into corners at the base of beads or, as shown in the bottom photos on the facing page, above a foot. There is more about this in chapter 10.

For concave curves, the long point of a skewed scraper is liable to catch. Instead, you need a round-nose scraper (see the photo at right).

Natural-edge rims are treated in exactly the same way, only much of the time you are turning space. As with the shaping cuts using the gouge, you need to decide the line the tool needs to take and move it along that line regardless of what is or isn't there. The edge strokes the wood but is not pushed into it.

To shear-scrape a concave curve, use a standard round-nose scraper on edge.

Working the Angles

So far this chapter has dealt with simple curves, but of course these are often used with wide rims or in combination to create angled profiles. Mostly the cuts to smooth these surfaces are much the same, although the angle of approach can be different and frequently against the grain. Typically you'll use fingernail-ground shallow gouges and scrapers to create the crisp angles and corners these forms produce. In the illustration on p. 126, you can see ways of working a few archetypal bowl forms.

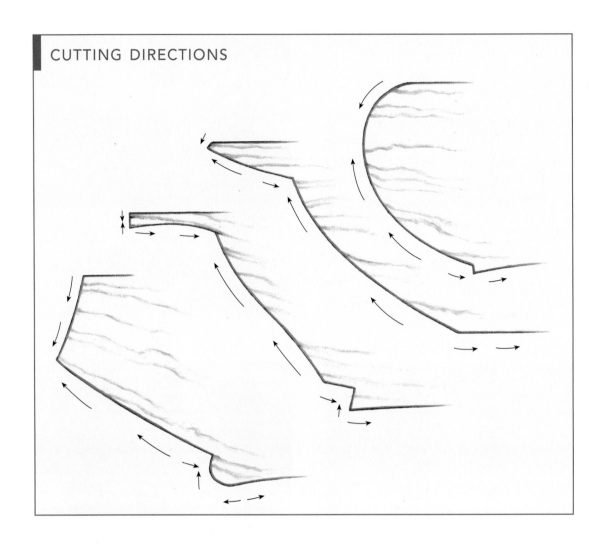

CUTTING DIRECTIONS

When turning a wide rim, you have most control of the gouge when cutting against the grain toward center. Go steadily, letting the wood come to the tool, and you'll usually get a clean cut.

When turning a wide rim, you have most control of the gouge when cutting against the grain toward center, as shown in the photo at left. If you make the cut steadily, letting the wood come to the tool rather than pushing the edge into the wood, you'll usually get a pretty good surface. Wide rims, particularly on smaller bowls, tend to be thin and therefore flexible, so be extra careful not to apply any bevel pressure against the wood (which should be minimal anyway). When scraping a wide rim, always shear-scrape rather than use the tool flat on the rest. And use a spear-point scraper into the corner.

Final Inspection

Before sanding and finishing, check the profile carefully, looking for torn grain and gauging the quality of your curves and any straight portions of your profile (cylinders and conical sections). You can easily check these using a straightedge, which for me is a powerful reason for avoiding straight lines in your work. You can't argue or have much fun with a straightedge.

Curves are much more forgiving and interesting, although they still need to flow without dips, bumps, or abrupt changes in direction. Such irregularities can usually be felt, but to be sure the line will be seen to flow in the finished bowl (the application of finish has a way of highlighting glumpfs), go over the surface with a piece of 240-grit sandpaper, backed by the palm of your hand. Any smoothed sections, as shown in the top photo at right, indicate bumps, which are usually best shear-scraped away—this can be very subtle!

Once you have a satisfactory surface off the tool, it's time to sand and finish. With experience you'll learn exactly when a surface is smooth enough to sand and what you can get away with. What you can expect of abrasives (and other aspects of finishing) is dealt with in chapter 9.

Completing the whole of the profile at this stage is not always a good idea. Often the bowl fails to remount accurately in preparation for hollowing, particularly if you are using screws and a faceplate. Typically I will sand and finish only the parts I won't be able to get at easily later. Thus a bowl mounted on a faceplate won't be sanded at all, while one with a foot will be finished about one-third the way up the profile, as shown in the top right photo on p. 121. If you are going to remount the bowl between centers to complete the base (see chapter 8), marking the center of the base with a pencil dot will make aligning the tail center easy.

The torn end grain on this camphor laurel bowl (top) will sand away with some effort; the surface could be cleaner, like that of the Tasmanian blackwood (above), but these slight tool and chatter marks present no sanding problems.

7 COMPLETING THE INSIDE

By the time you get to hollowing a bowl, most of the work is done and the design decisions largely made, apart from determining the precise wall thickness and shape of the rim. The lathe can generally be run slightly faster than when roughing out the form, but you should still proceed with care, bearing in mind the recommended speeds given in the chart on p. 13. Working with roughed-out bowls, there's little left to remove, but making these final cuts and leaving a smooth surface off the tool is always a challenge. And the challenge increases the thinner the bowl wall becomes. When turning a translucent bowl, keep the speed lower yet, for two reasons: First, centrifugal force is liable to split the wood, especially if it's green. Second, if the wood vibrates or distorts, that is less of a problem at lower speeds because everything happens more slowly.

In this chapter, I'll look at how to complete the internal turning in three sections: working in from the rim, smoothing the midsection, and fairing the bottom. Each portion of the inside curve presents different problems. But first let's consider what needs to be done to the profile and the rim before you complete the hollowing.

Remounting the Bowl and Truing the Form

If the chuck is enclosing a foot, a piece of soft cloth between the two, as shown in the photo below, limits any bruising of the wood. Damage is a serious problem only when the foot is larger than the true diameter of the jaws, in which case the jaw corners can leave eight marks on the

A soft cloth helps protect the finish-turned wood from the chuck jaws when the foot is slightly oversize.

*You need true only the upper profile
since the prime concern is how the rim will look.*

When expanding jaws within a foot, grip on as wide a diameter as possible for maximum support. The width of the material around the jaws should be at least 15 percent of the bowl diameter.

These long jaws grip on a 1¾-in. (45mm) diameter. Located in a groove as on this small outflowing bowl, any bruising of the wood is difficult to find.

foot. When the chuck jaws are located in a groove, as shown in the top photo at right, any bruising is difficult to find.

If your bowl is held by an expanding collet, as shown in the photo above, remember that the bowl is not as secure as it would be if the jaws gripped around a foot. The width of the band around the jaws should be at least 15 percent of the bowl diameter.

It is not unusual for the rim to run slightly out of true once the bowl is remounted. If adjusting it in the chuck has no effect, the eccentricity might be due to some slight warping or the result of heavy sanding when completing the profile. What you should do about this depends on the extent of the eccentricity and the intended shape of the rim. If the rim is only slightly off center and to be rounded over,

A symmetrical rim needs to run true; otherwise it will be thicker in some places than others and look inept. Camphor laurel, 11 in. by 4 in. (280mm by 100mm).

The upper section of an enclosed form is easiest to shear-cut and complete when the bowl is remounted for hollowing.

you can live with it. A symmetrical rim with hard edges like that shown in the bottom photo on p. 129 needs to run absolutely true; otherwise, variations in thickness will look odd and out of control.

To true the upper part of the profile on outflowing forms, use a very delicate shear cut, working from the left toward the rim. This approach is particularly appropriate on thinner outflowing bowls, where the bowl wall might flex slightly, in that you start cutting with the bevel rubbing. In contrast, it is difficult to see the precise orbit of a rim when cutting in from the right, and any flexing increases the likelihood of a catch.

Enclosed forms can be cut from the right (see the photo at left) because they are stronger and less likely to flex when the edge contacts

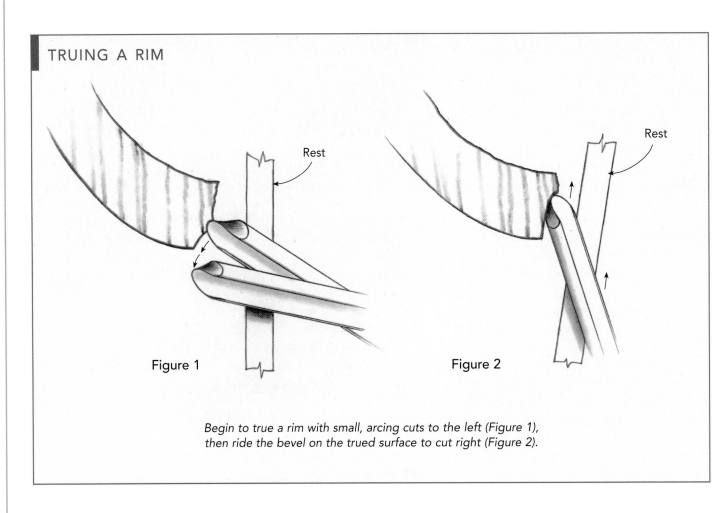

TRUING A RIM

Figure 1

Figure 2

Rest

Rest

Begin to true a rim with small, arcing cuts to the left (Figure 1), then ride the bevel on the trued surface to cut right (Figure 2).

Always true the rim before you start to cut the inner wall. I use small, arcing cuts to the left and a shear-cut to the right.

the wood. You complete the upper profile with the form held by the base because the cuts are easier from the right.

You need true only the upper profile since the prime concern is how the rim will look. Eccentric surfaces just below the rim blend during sanding, and it takes a very fine sense of touch or a micrometer to detect where the wall varies in thickness.

You need to true the top of the rim before you start hollowing, as shown in the photos above, starting with small arcing cuts (see the illustration on the facing page). Don't bother with final shaping of wide rims at this stage in case you have a catch as you start on the inner curve.

Before you start hollowing, it helps to establish the final internal depth, so you can see how far you have to go. One way is to drill a hole at center on a drill press, where you can set the depth precisely. However, I usually do this by hand and eye on the lathe using a depth drill as I did at the rough-hollowing stage (see the photo on p. 89). Either way, once the hole is

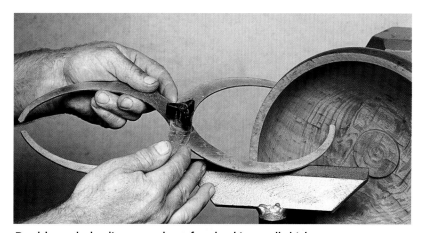

Double-ended calipers are best for checking wall thickness.

drilled, I open the center so that as I cut the internal curve I can see where I am heading. Alternatively, you can use rulers and measure the inside and outside to calculate the bottom thickness, or check as you go using double-ended calipers, as shown in the photo above.

How thick or thin the wall and bottom might be and how it affects the overall balance and feel of a bowl is discussed in the afterword and in my book *Turned Bowl Design* (The Taunton Press, 1987).

A gouge (whether shallow, as shown here, or deep-fluted) enters the wood on its side with the bevel pointing in the direction you want to go. Keep your hand on the rest with your thumb also on the rest to provide a stop and fulcrum for the tool, while your forefinger supports the bowl wall behind the cut.

Initial Cuts and the Rim

My strategy for completing the inside of a bowl is to use a gouge to shear-cut as far as possible around the curve with the bevel rubbing the wood, then use scrapers across the bottom. On open forms, having the bevel rub all the way to center is easy enough, but I still prefer to use scrapers toward the center because I have greater control over the depth of the cut than when using a gouge, even though the surface quality might not be as good as I might wish.

You should complete initial cuts establishing the wall thickness for about 1 in. (25mm) before you finish any detailing on the rim and continue the cut toward the base. A smaller, lighter gouge is preferable when cutting in from the rim, especially on bowls less than 10 in. (250mm) in diameter, because you can feel what is happening through the tool. Start the cut with the gouge on its side and the bevel

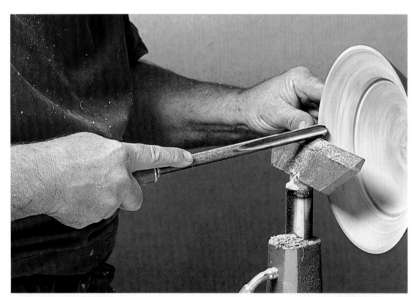

Once the nose of the gouge is in the wood, rotate the tool slightly counterclockwise for a better shaving. As the tool cuts down the wall, move your thumb with the tool blade along the rest (right). Have your right hand near the ferrule and the handle under your arm against your side for maximum control (above).

pointing in the direction you want to go, as shown in the top photo on the facing page. Keep your hand on the rest with your thumb providing a stop and fulcrum for the tool while your forefinger supports the bowl wall at the back of the cut. If the profile is not finished, a light sanding with 100-grit abrasive reduces the friction on your forefinger and consequently any heat buildup.

Once the nose of the gouge is in the wood, you can rotate the tool slightly counterclockwise for a better shaving, just as when roughing out the bowl. As the tool cuts down the wall, your thumb needs to move with the tool blade along the rest (see the bottom photos on the facing page).

I like a long bevel so that the handle lies at an angle where I can keep some of my weight over it as it enters the wood, as shown in the bottom left photo on the facing page. A steep bevel can mean that at the start of the cut the handle is pointing away from you, making it very difficult to hold firmly, especially if the form is enclosed.

The entry cut on an enclosed form follows the same principles, only using a narrow gouge with a very long bevel (see the top photo at right). The long bevel makes it possible to shear-cut almost across the axis, but holding the tool and seeing what you're doing can be a problem. To make the entry cut, you need to lean right across the lathe bed.

Completing the inside of a natural-edge bowl is exactly the same, as shown in the bottom photo at right, except that you must keep the tool on a steady trajectory, so that although the wood is intermittent, you'll still cut a smooth surface on what wood there is. You don't want any tool pressure against the wood, otherwise it will flex and you'll get chatter and tool marks that will have to be sanded away. Natural edges look best when of even thickness. Aim to cut past the bark section in one go for the smoothest line.

Using a long bevel, you can shear-cut back under the rim of an enclosed form, although holding the tool and seeing what you're doing can be a problem. To make the entry cut, you need to lean right across the lathe bed.

When turning a natural edge, you have to keep the tool on a steady trajectory to ensure you cut a smooth surface on what wood there is. Natural edges look best when of even thickness. For the smoothest line, aim to cut past the bark section in one pass.

On wide-rimmed bowls, turn the approximate shape, then mark the line of the profile on the face and work in relation to that line.

FINISHING CUTS ON A WIDE RIM

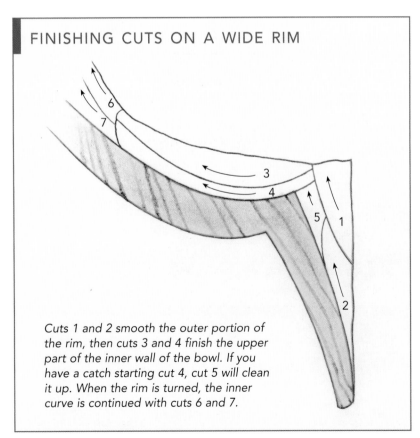

Cuts 1 and 2 smooth the outer portion of the rim, then cuts 3 and 4 finish the upper part of the inner wall of the bowl. If you have a catch starting cut 4, cut 5 will clean it up. When the rim is turned, the inner curve is continued with cuts 6 and 7.

On wide-rimmed bowls, turn the approximate shape as shown in the photo at left above, then mark the line of the profile on the face (see the photo at right above) and work in relation to that reference line. Don't mark where you intend to make the entry cut because you'll lose that point of reference the first time you enter there. Cut the inner curve first, gauging wall thickness from the profile line, then finish the rim as shown in the illustration at left.

Cutting the Midsection Wall

Continue the cuts onto the midsection of the inner wall only after you have turned the rim. If the bowl is more than 6 in. (150mm) in diameter, transfer to a heavier and stronger ½-in. (13mm) bowl gouge that won't flex as you work further over the rest. If there is a substantial shoulder of waste partway down the wall, you need to hold the tool firmly on the rest and

When completing roughed bowls, mark any ultrathin areas with pencil while the lathe is running, so you can be sure not to cut too much there.

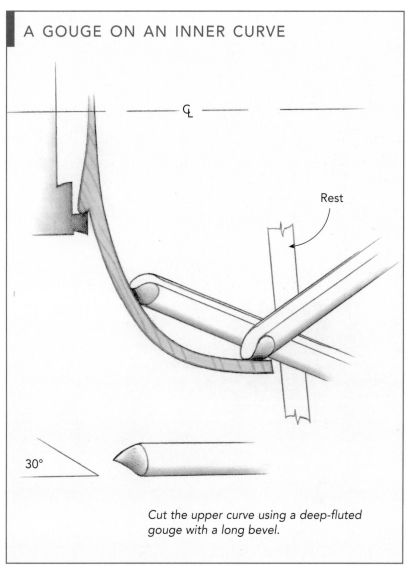

A GOUGE ON AN INNER CURVE

Rest

30°

Cut the upper curve using a deep-fluted gouge with a long bevel.

make entry cuts into that waste just as you did on the rim. You might need several cuts on larger bowls before you can continue the surface already established.

When finishing roughed bowls, there are often areas where there isn't much wood to play with, particularly in the corner of the remounting shoulder that located the chuck. Mark any problematic corners with pencil while the lathe is running (see the photo above). Occasionally off-center warping will leave you with a wider patch where the wall is already as thin as you want (or even thinner). Highlight these with pencil marks (with the lathe off); these show as a broad gray line when the wood is spinning. Then aim to achieve a flowing curve without removing the lines or marks, or remove as little wood as possible where they are located until

the last possible moment. Where the bowl wall is extremely thin, a safer way of completing the job is to use power-sanding to blend in the thin patch with the thicker surrounding wall, starting with 60-grit abrasive (see p. 161).

The thinner you turn a bowl wall, the more it can flex. Any tool pressure against the wood will set up a vibration as it forces the wall out of

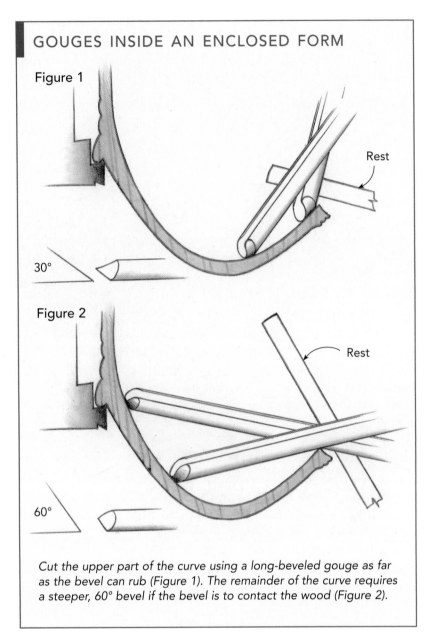

GOUGES INSIDE AN ENCLOSED FORM

Figure 1

30°

Rest

Figure 2

60°

Rest

Cut the upper part of the curve using a long-beveled gouge as far as the bevel can rub (Figure 1). The remainder of the curve requires a steeper, 60° bevel if the bevel is to contact the wood (Figure 2).

The best surface is obtained from an edge presented at about 45 degrees to the oncoming wood.

true. You want the bevel only touching the wood, not forced against it. Better still, support the wood at the back of the tool, as shown in the photo at right on p. 132. Here the bowl wall passes between your finger and the tool like a board through a thickness planer. The finger equalizes the pressure exerted by the gouge, so if your finger gets too hot you are pushing the tool too hard against the wood. You can also wear a glove, although a handful of shavings is probably more effective at dissipating the heat.

As usual, the best surface is obtained when the portion of the edge cutting is presented at about 45 degrees to the oncoming wood. The gouges I use have a rounded left wing, which enables me to use the back cut much as on the profile (see the photo at right on p. 118), although I still need to be wary of catching the edge on the tight curves of small, enclosed forms. Don't use the deep gouge flute up on enclosed forms until you've cut around the bend and are working toward the base.

As you cut, keep an eye on the final depth (assuming you've drilled and widened a depth hole). Try to move with the tool, keeping your weight over the handle whenever possible. With all these cuts, the handle is under my forearm for most of the cut. I have my hand nearer the end of the handle only when near the bottom of bowls where I'm cutting more than 6 in. (150mm) over the rest.

Gauging wall thickness is a problem at this stage and it is easy to cut the wrong line. If you cut too deeply, you can go through the side, although you'll realize what might happen before it actually does. If possible, take another cut from the rim and thin the upper wall, even marking the corner as shown in the photo on p. 135. Fortunately a bowl can get pretty thin and still hang together—and look good, too—if you can maintain a smooth internal curve.

However, it's common for most turners to err on the side of caution and not cut away enough, which makes for a chunky, physically unbalanced form. It is better to turn an even wall thickness, slim it in the midsection, or taper the wall evenly all the way from the bottom.

Double-ended calipers are best for checking wall thickness to see how things are going. Always stop the lathe before using any calipers (see the bottom photo on p. 131).

Cylindrical sides are best cut using a heavy shallow gouge with a long bevel. On internal corners, roll the tool on its side to avoid catching the edge, as shown in the photo at right.

When turning a very thin wall or working green wood, completely sand the profile before any hollowing. This reduces the friction against your finger to a minimum, but, more importantly, it establishes a surface to which you can relate the inside.

Turn very thin bowls with the lathe running slower rather than faster. Higher speeds lead to greater problems with vibration and chatter marks, and the centrifugal forces can explode the bowl.

Very thin walls are best turned in a series of steps from the rim in, so there is support from the thicker wall below. If you're working dry and stable wood, this should present few problems. You leave sanding until the turning is completed. Turning green wood is a different matter because it warps almost as soon as it's turned. You cannot take your time, and you need to work quickly and positively. Again, the rim is the most crucial area, so once that and the top of the curve are cut, you can accommodate a small amount of warping.

Green wood is much easier to work than dry, so turning most of the curve is not so difficult. Just take a deep breath and go for it. There's more on turning green wood on p. 142.

Cylindrical sides are best cut using a shallow long-beveled gouge. When cutting into a corner, roll the tool on its side to avoid catching the edge.

Across the Bottom

To remove the bulk of the waste across the bottom of a bowl, I use a bowl gouge (see the photo on p. 138). In deep bowls you need a steep bevel if bevel contact is to be maintained with the wood (see the illustration on p. 138) to see how long- and steep-beveled gouges work on the inside of an enclosed form).

Remember that the nearer you get to center, the slower the rate at which you can move the edge into the cut. As always, have the portion of the edge cutting at about 45 degrees to the oncoming wood. On open forms, try to keep the gouge pointing toward center so you can steer into center.

Across the bottom there is always the possibility that you'll go too deep and go through or make the base too thin to be practical. On the other hand, you don't want it too thick and heavy, so it pays to check the exact depth with

She-Oak Bowl

Intended as a sushi dish, this bowl would also be ideal as a container for dumping keys and small change or jewelry. Such flat bowls are most easily hollowed using square-end scrapers, then finished with a shallow gouge.

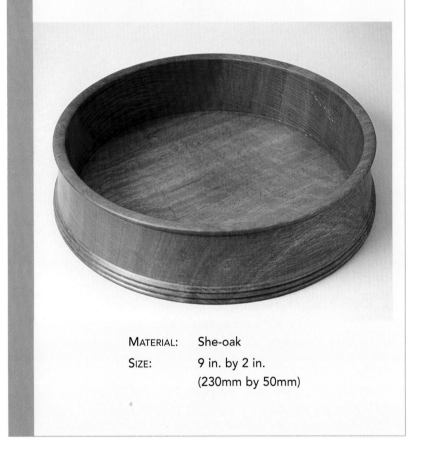

MATERIAL:	She-oak
SIZE:	9 in. by 2 in. (230mm by 50mm)

A heavy deep-fluted bowl gouge is the best tool both for removing the bulk of the waste and for cutting the final curve.

Although gouges will usually leave a cleaner surface across the bottom, I prefer to use scrapers for the final cuts because I feel I have greater control over cutting exactly the curve I want.

Scrapers inside Bowls

Scrapers are wonderful finishing tools if handled properly, but they can also be involved in some of the worst catches.

I try never to use scrapers near the rim of a thin-walled open bowl, because catching the edge and severely torn grain is a near certainty. Before showing you how scrapers can be used, I'll look at what happens when they catch, why the catches are so bad, and how they can be avoided.

Catches and the resulting damage are always worse on open bowls. Consider how easily the rim of a plastic bowl can be distorted. That's why most of the plastic tubs that contain the yogurt, screws, honey, or wax polishes we buy have a strengthening rim.

Although stiffer, wood reacts to pressure in the same way, so if you put any pressure against a bowl as it spins, it starts oscillating as you push it out of round, pulsing either side of its

calipers. If you still have a way to go, it is important to keep track of exactly where you are in relation to the underside of the bowl and especially any recess in the base. Once I know the thickness of the base, I work toward the final surface, leaving a small mesa at center as a point of reference until the rest of the internal curve is completed.

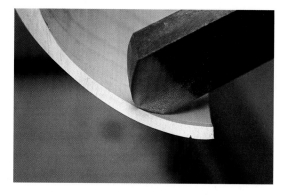

The cutaway bowl wall lets us see that, in contrast with the scraper kept flat on the rest, an edge tilted to shear-scrape presents very little metal in the horizontal plane.

true course. When a portion flexing inward hits the horizontal edge of a scraper, as shown in the illustration at right, the area of contact between the two can more than double, along with the force between bowl and tool.

Scrapers can be used flat, or they can be tilted on edge to shear-scrape. On open bowls, the nearer you work to the base and center, the less the bowl wall distorts and the more useful scrapers become. The broader the edge you present to the wood, the bigger and nastier the catch you risk, especially near the rim where flexing and vibration occur most. In the photos above, the cutaway bowl wall lets you see that an edge tilted to shear-scrape presents virtually no metal in the horizontal plane, in contrast with the scraper kept flat on the rest.

SCRAPERS NEAR THE RIM

Never use a scraper flat in the upper half of a bowl unless the wall thickness is more than one-fifth of the bowl's diameter, and even then proceed with caution because catches, when they happen, are usually heavy. Lowering the speed to about 20 percent of those recommended in the speed chart on p. 13 helps, too, reducing vibration and consequently the risk of a catch.

To scrape the upper sections of a thin bowl, reduce the lathe speed to about 300 rpm and tilt the tool on edge to shear-scrape, as shown in the top right photo on p. 140. Very thin

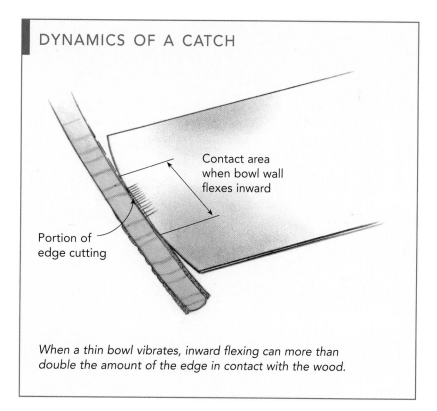

DYNAMICS OF A CATCH

Contact area when bowl wall flexes inward

Portion of edge cutting

When a thin bowl vibrates, inward flexing can more than double the amount of the edge in contact with the wood.

green wood is so flexible that it can be shear-scraped at very low speeds using exactly the same technique.

For enclosed forms or tight curves, use a narrow round-nose scraper on edge (see the top left photo on p. 140). When the edge is tilted up to shear-scrape, it exerts very little pressure against the wood and rarely catches if the portion of the edge in contact with the wood is nearly in line with the fulcrum.

Shear-scraping is the safest way to clean up the upper sections of a bowl, especially a thin one. Reduce the lathe speed to about 300 rpm and use a round-nose scraper tilted on edge.

I find curves come more easily when I use scrapers with a radius that is only slightly tighter than the curve I'm cutting.

SCRAPERS IN THE LOWER HALF

In the lower half of a bowl, there is substantially less vibration than up toward the rim, and you can use the scrapers flat with less likelihood of a catch. You can remove a lot of wood within the diameter supported by the chuck by pushing the tool straight in in a series of steps. This is particularly useful when you need to refine the thickness of the base or turn a flattish bottom, as shown in the photo on the facing page.

To blend the gouge-cut surfaces into the bottom, move the scraper in a series of arcs so the edge just brushes the surface to produce a very thin curly shaving, as shown in the center photo at left and the illustration on the facing page. A scraper with as broad a curve as possible for the curve you want to cut is much easier to use than a tight-radius round-nose scraper, which does not relate so well to the curve being cut. Nevertheless, do not use more than ½ in. (13mm) of the edge at one time. For a finer surface, use the same sweeping cuts more gently so you remove only dust, as shown in the bottom

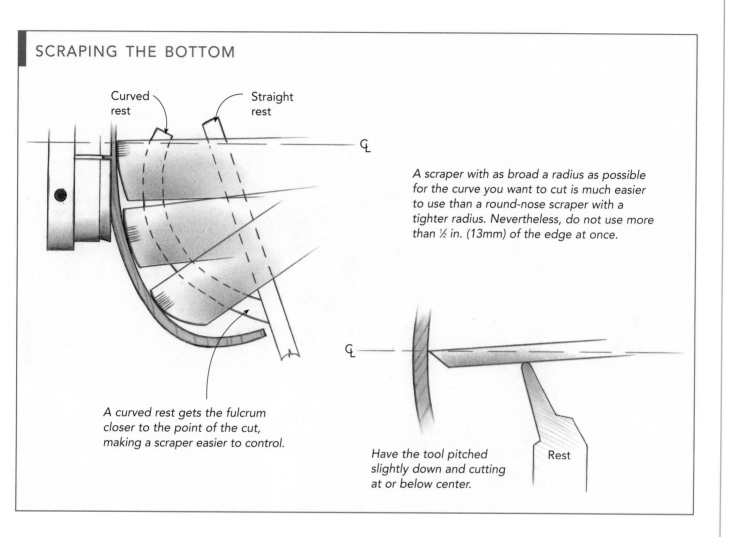

SCRAPING THE BOTTOM

Curved rest

Straight rest

A scraper with as broad a radius as possible for the curve you want to cut is much easier to use than a round-nose scraper with a tighter radius. Nevertheless, do not use more than ½ in. (13mm) of the edge at once.

A curved rest gets the fulcrum closer to the point of the cut, making a scraper easier to control.

Have the tool pitched slightly down and cutting at or below center.

Rest

photo on the facing page. Always have the tool pitched slightly down, especially when cutting at center or on a flat surface. Away from center on an internal curve, work slightly above center so that in the event of a catch, the tool carries into space.

Because the fibers lie lengthwise across the bottom of a bowl, scraping tends to leave a rougher surface than a gouge but a more flowing, less undulating curve. Bumps and dips are difficult to get rid of, so I go for the overall shape even though it might not be as well cut. Sanding soon makes the surface smooth.

A cylindrical bowl with a flat bottom is best cut using scrapers (see the photo at right) at because of the difficulties shearing with a gouge

Across a flat or slightly convex bottom, scrapers do the job best. For these cuts, nominally straight scrapers should be very slightly radiused, so only a portion of the edge can contact the wood at one time.

Tasmanian Myrtle Bowls

These shapes are reminiscent of Southwest Native American pottery or perhaps the calabash bowls of Hawaii. Such traditional forms always provide a good starting point.

MATERIAL:	Tasmanian myrtle
SIZES:	8¼ in. by 3¾ in. (210mm by 95mm), 4 in. by 2¾ in. (120mm by 70mm)

Scraping tends to leave a rougher surface across the base than a gouge but a more flowing, less undulating curve.

in this situation. Across most of the bottom, I use a square-end scraper, which in fact has a very slight radius to keep it from catching on a flat surface. I use a skewed scraper into the corner.

Green-Turned Bowls

Turning green wood to completion, creating a green-turned bowl, always seems to attract special attention, as if there's something radically different about working freshly felled timber. Green wood is full of sap, even in the winter when the moisture is at its lowest, so be prepared to get very wet working it.

The techniques for working wet wood are exactly the same as for dry, only the wood generally works more easily and with fatter shavings. There's a long tradition in many parts of the world for turning utilitarian bowls from unseasoned logs. Even though the woods used were known for their stability, the bowls might still warp a bit, but so what? The base could be

A bright light behind the wood can help you judge the wood's thickness as you turn, although water in the wood transmits light and makes the wall appear thinner than it is.

The techniques for working wet wood are exactly the same as for dry, only the wood generally works more easily and with fatter shavings.

flattened if this was an issue, but generally it wasn't by all accounts. In the late 1970s, I began turning thin bowls from freshly felled holly, using its well-known tendency to warp dramatically to create wavy bowls similar to those shown in the top photo at right. The trick with these is having the confidence to make the final internal cuts within a few seconds before the form warps. Sanding is a slight problem because sanding a warping bowl is awkward at the best of times, and wet wood doesn't like being sanded at all, although it soon dries out.

To make these wavy bowls, you need very fresh wood that is known to warp. You can test this by putting a small sample bowl—such as the 4-in. (100mm)-diameter bowls pictured in the bottom photo at right—in a microwave oven for one minute on maximum cook. The bowl should come out too hot to hold and already warped, if other bowls from the same material are going to warp at all. To get symmetrical forms, the blank should be cut from straight, even-grained timber devoid of knots with the pith on the top of the bowl.

A bright light on the other side of the wood, as shown in the photo at right on the facing page, is a great aid to working thin, though you must account for the false impression given by the water in the wood transmitting light, which makes the bowl appear thinner than it is. When you think you are almost through the wall, you've probably got it just about right.

Completing bowls in freshly felled wood is exhilarating. Ninety seconds in a microwave oven on full power induced this bowl to dry and warp instantly. Eucalyptus burl, 5¼ in. (135mm) in diameter.

To test how much these 4-in. (100mm) casuarina bowls would warp, I put them in a microwave oven for one minute on full power. Although the bases have gone oval, they remain almost flat.

8 COMPLETING THE BASE

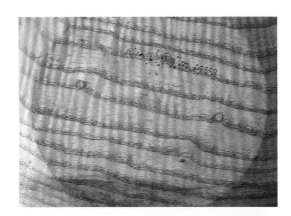

A bowl base with plugged screw holes is not as aesthetically pleasing as one without.

I n the small country workshop where I began my turning career, all bowls were made using screw faceplates. We filled the two screw holes in the base of each bowl with plastic wood. There were few attempts to remove evidence of how the bowl had been fixed on the lathe, but at least we sanded and polished our bases. A good many turners of those times covered their rough bases and unplugged holes with a layer of baize (a coarse woolen or cotton fabric resembling felt). In theory the baize was there to protect any furniture on which the bowl might sit, but it's a convenient way to hide sloppy work.

For years I remounted roughed bowls for completion on two #14 wood screws that penetrated the wood about $\frac{7}{16}$ in. (11mm), flattening the base on a coarse belt sander before attaching the faceplate. The wider the faceplate, the better support for the bowl and the shorter the screws you can use. A medium-sized bowl can easily be held using two $\frac{3}{8}$-in. (9mm) screws, provided the faceplate's diameter is about 40 percent of the bowl's diameter. Once sanding was complete, I filled the screw holes with plastic wood and sanded the base smooth with 180 grit on a belt sander. The big problem with this technique is keeping the base in the same plane as the bowl rim. It's easy for bowls to develop a lean, and it's difficult to rectify the problem. If you rechuck the bowl by the rim and turn the base, you know your bowl will stand upright.

Eliminating screw holes or chuck marks from the bottom of a bowl definitely enhances the overall quality of the piece. However, well into the 1980s, neatly plugged holes were par, and I put labels over them so they had very little impact at the point of sale. Years later, I still have some of those salad bowls to remind me of how we used to do things. Turning the bases was always an option, but at the time that added 20 percent to the wholesale price and most markets wouldn't bear the extra cost.

Things have come a long way since then, the self-centering four-jaw chucks revolutionizing how we can go about making bowls. Green baize on the base of a bowl is now mostly viewed as a sign of ineptitude, of poor work being covered. If you need to protect furniture from your bowls, three or four small, self-adhesive felt discs readily purchased at most hardware stores are the preferred option.

A more extreme school of thought insists that no bowl should ever retain any evidence of how it was fixed to the lathe and that all rabbets, feet, nubs, or grooves you might have grabbed with a chuck should go. I think retention of a fixing point is not a bad thing, especially if you need to refinish a bowl at some later date; being able to remount it on the lathe makes the job a whole lot easier.

There are also times when you might want to alter the profile because the original concept doesn't look too good, as shown in the top photo at right. The form looks better without the foot, as you can see in the bottom photo at right.

For the many occasions when you might want to rework a base or foot, you have three basic options for rechucking. Open forms need to fit into a chuck to be gripped by the rim, whereas any bowl with an undercut inner lip

There are often times when a profile looks better without the foot, so even if the foot is nicely finished, consider risking your bowl to end up with a better object. Tasmanian myrtle, 6 in. (150mm) diameter.

can be mounted over a chuck. In each case, you can use tail-center support for security. Ultrathin and bark-rimmed bowls are best mounted between centers so there is minimal pressure against the rim.

Whenever you remount a turned form, there is the possibility that it won't run true or as true as you'd like. Wood is not as stable as metal or plastic, or as even in density, so there are a number of reasons why you will have to come to terms with eccentric surfaces. As when tru-

Burl Bowls

These bowls were not dissimilar when turned, but while I completed the one on the left from a roughed bowl that had seasoned, I turned the one on the right (with a rounded base) to completion from green wood, knowing that it would warp.

MATERIALS: Tasmanian myrtle (left),
eucalyptus burl (right)

SIZES: 6 in. by 4 in.
(150mm by 100mm) (left),
5⅛ in. by 3½ in.
(130mm by 90mm) (right)

ing up a rim before completing the inside (see pp. 128-131), you turn your new surface as near as possible to the old, then blend the two together with abrasives.

There are a number of different approaches to remounting bowls for completing the base. But before looking at the ways mechanical chucks can be used, let's take a look at how low-cost homemade options can be made from scrap or roughed bowls.

Jam Chucks

The photo essay on pp. 148–149 shows the basic sequence for turning the base of a bowl. In this case, the enclosed bowl fits over a shoulder in a chuck turned from a piece of 1¼-in. (32mm) medium-density fiberboard (MDF).

First, measure the diameter that will fit the chuck, in this case to the inner lip of the rim. In steps 1 and 2 on p. 148, note how my left fingers locate one point of the dividers on the rim so I can watch the other point as I adjust it. Transfer this measurement to the face of the chuck (how to do this is shown on p. 114).

The shoulder or tenon can be turned using a square-end scraper, but I always use a shallow gouge, taking the opportunity to practice my entry cuts when a catch doesn't matter (see Step 3 on p. 148). The secret to getting a secure fit is turning a very shallow taper on the shoulder into which or over which the bowl is fitting. Think in terms of one degree. Pushing the bowl over or into the chuck should create a slight grating noise. If the taper is too steep, the bowl will jam on quickly and unjam just as quickly. The rim of the bowl should sit against the chuck as shown in Figure 1 of the illustration on the facing page for maximum security and easy centering. A bowl fitted into a chuck as shown in Figures 2 and 3 is held more securely, but it is difficult to ensure that the rim is in contact with the bottom of the chuck because you cannot see what's happening inside.

Theoretically, symmetrical bowls will mount accurately, but typically, heavy sanding or slight warping will have distorted the rim enough that the bowl is slightly out of true. Watch the top horizon of the bowl (the far side) as you spin it by hand a few times. When it's pitched away from you, give the opposite side of the bottom a glancing tap to pull it into true. The shallower the taper of the chuck shoulder, the easier adjustments are to make.

JAM CHUCKS

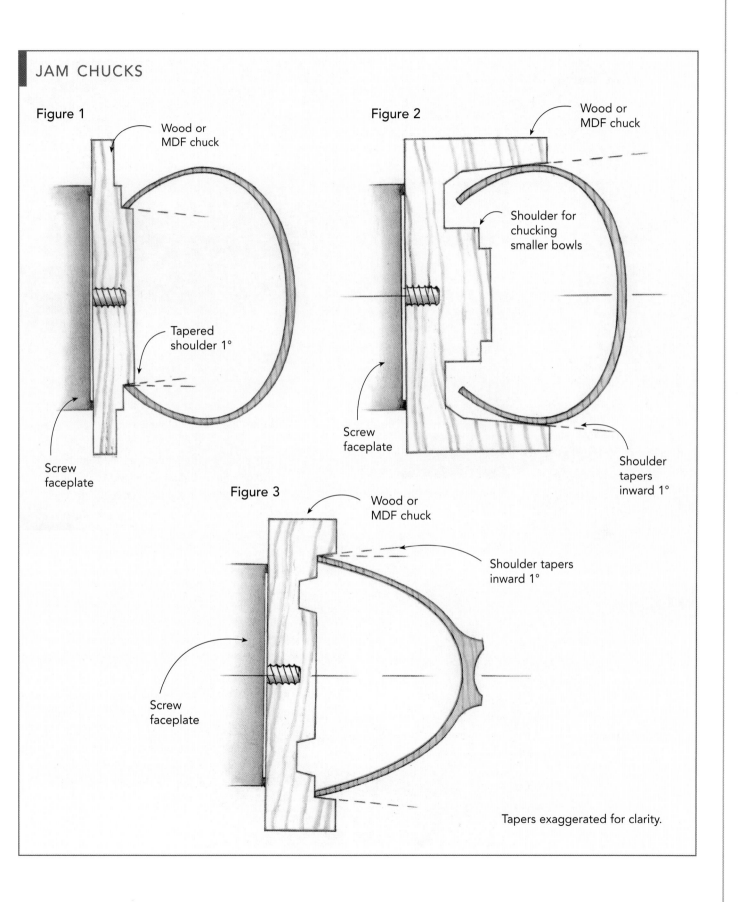

Figure 1

Wood or MDF chuck

Tapered shoulder 1°

Screw faceplate

Figure 2

Wood or MDF chuck

Shoulder for chucking smaller bowls

Screw faceplate

Shoulder tapers inward 1°

Figure 3

Wood or MDF chuck

Shoulder tapers inward 1°

Screw faceplate

Tapers exaggerated for clarity.

Jam Chuck Simplicity

A simple and inexpensive way to remount a bowl so you can finish the base is to turn a jam chuck, which will hold the bowl by friction. Tap the bowl gently into or over the chuck until it runs true. Use the tail center for extra security.

1 Measure the diameter of the bowl.

2 Mark the diameter on the jam chuck.

3 Cut a light taper into the chuck. Think in terms of 1 degree. Make the bottom of the shoulder slightly fatter than the top so the bowl fits onto the tenon with a slight grating sound.

4 Mount the bowl, then use a ⅜-in. (9mm) shallow gouge and small arcing cuts to remove the waste around the rim of the foot, working from smaller to larger diameter.

5 Then turn the base slightly concave, cutting toward center from the rim.

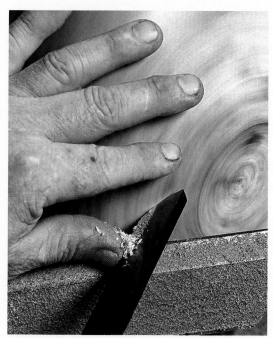

6 Complete the profile with a shear-scrape, and blend the new surface with the old.

7 Finally, complete the base. Here I use the scraper corner to create a small rabbet-like detail.

TURNING THE BASE

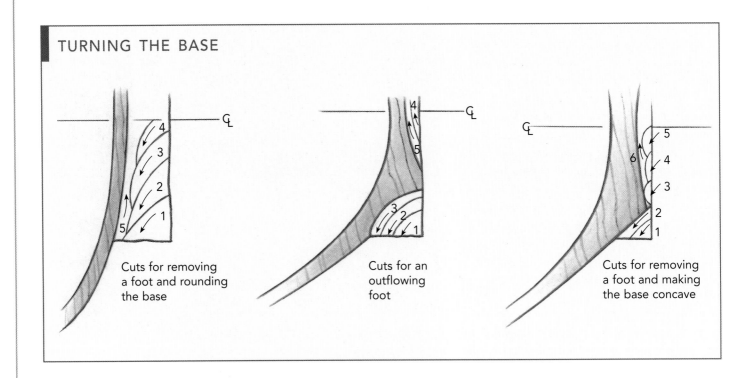

Cuts for removing
a foot and rounding
the base

Cuts for an
outflowing
foot

Cuts for removing
a foot and making
the base concave

A flat tail center is
useful when the base
is thin or finished.
Flat centers are com-
mercially available,
but it's easy to turn
your own to fit over
your conical or cup
centers.

If you have a variable-speed control, slow the
lathe slightly for the turning so that when the
bowl comes loose (as it will sooner or later) the
experience is less exciting. Go down one speed
with step pulleys. As work proceeds, it pays to
keep your left hand across the bottom of the
bowl as well as on the rest, where your thumb
provides a lateral fulcrum on the rest for the
gouge (see Step 4 on p. 149). Then if the bowl
does come loose, it will rattle around in or on
the chuck without flying off, while you hit the
off switch. (This is when you need a readily
accessible off switch that you can reach without
using your hands.)

Remove the waste—in this case the foot—with
a series of small arcing cuts, as shown in the
illustration above, before working from the rim
of the base toward center (see Step 5 on p. 149).
The main reason for a bowl coming loose is
making a cut toward the center too fast for the
speed of the wood. The wood is moving ever
slower as you near the center, so you must

reduce the pace at which you move the tool forward the nearer center you get. Otherwise, the wood will roll up the tool edge and the bowl will be levered from the chuck. Use a series of small arcing cuts away from center to remove the bulk of the waste, then make a very light and slow final shear cut into center. Better still is to complete the base as much as possible earlier, while completing the profile, when the job is more securely fixed on the lathe.

Once the waste is gone, finish smoothing the surface using a shear scraper very gently (see Step 6 on p. 149), or start sanding. I like to detail the base, which is most simply done by easing the corner of the shear scraper into the wood, as shown in Step 7 on p. 149 (see also the photos on p. 169).

You can use tail-center support, but of course this prevents access to the center as well as damages it. You can use a flat center, as shown in the photo on the facing page, but this further limits access near center. Tail-center support does allow you to work with greater confidence, although I rarely use it. If you have a nub remaining at center, it's easy to remove it and finish by hand off the lathe.

Removing a bowl from a jam chuck can be a problem because when fitted properly a seal is created and suction keeps bowl and chuck together. The simplest way to release the bowl is to tap the chuck with a heavy instrument, which breaks the seal and frees the bowl (see the top photo at right). If this fails, unwind the chuck and tap its rim against the lathe bed until the bowl drops free.

Rechucking between Centers

Bowls with an uneven rim and no possible fixing point on the inside or bowls full of holes can be mounted over a rounded form with tail-

If a bowl is difficult to remove from a jam chuck, firmly tap the chuck with something heavy, and the bowl should drop free.

This thin box elder bowl being mounted over a bowl profile with tail-center support is wrapped in cling wrap to keep it from flying apart.

Putting a dot at center when you're completing the profile makes centering a bowl over a vacuum chuck or between centers easy—just align the dot with the tail center.

A ⅜-in. (9mm) shallow gouge is the best tool for working across the base and around the tail-center cone.

center support (see the center photo on p. 151). The disadvantage is that you might have to finish the center of the base off the lathe by hand, but that's not a big deal.

I have several rounded forms of different diameters turned from MDF that I mount on a screw chuck just like my jam-fit chucks. A piece of soft cloth goes between the bowl and the drive to protect the finished surface. The cloth is a well-used finishing rag full of wax and oil, the stickiness of which helps prevent the bowl from slipping, but if it does slip, the inside gets a little extra polishing.

The bowl shown in the center photo on p. 151 is thin and very fragile, so I wrapped it in cling wrap to make sure it didn't fly apart. I folded the surplus cling wrap around the rim inwards, and there was enough to separate the bowl and chuck. The depth of this bowl demanded a long chuck, so I use a roughed bowl mounted over large step jaws.

You can get very good at centering bowls over a chuck by eye, but it's easier to mark center when you're completing the profile. Then all you have to do is align the dot at center with the

You can get very good at centering bowls over a chuck by eye,
but it's easier to mark center when you're completing the profile.

tail center, as shown in the photo at left on the facing page.

With the job firmly between centers as shown in the bottom photo on p. 151, no special cutting techniques are required until you are almost done. The photos at right on the facing page show the ⅜-in. (9mm) shallow gouge in action across the base. Once the finish is applied, you can use the gouge right on its side to undercut the wood around the center, but it's safer to complete the base off the lathe using a sanding pad mounted on the lathe.

Mechanical Chucks

Most commercially available chucks offer an optional set of bowl jaws with adjustable buttons enabling you to grip a wide range of rims so you can turn the base (see the top photo at right). These chucks offer huge flexibility over the jam chucks you turn yourself, eliminating all the fiddling around trying to cut a recess or tenon just right. Most large jaws have eight buttons, but since button changing is a bit tedious in production, I often have them set in fours so I can accommodate two ranges of bowls.

Another option is to forget the buttons and make some jaws in MDF like those shown in the photo at right, and turn shoulders to fit your bowls. This is especially useful for production work, and if you turn the shoulder with the jaws wide open, you increase the range over which they can grip without the corners of the jaw bearing on the bowl.

You can mount small enclosed bowls over expanding chuck jaws, or use the shoulder as I

Bowl jaws provide by far the most secure grip for turning the base. The red buttons can be relocated on different diameters for smaller bowls.

On these smaller bowl jaws, I've replaced the buttons with MDF cut to match the jaws. By opening the jaws wide before turning the recess, I extend the range over which the chuck can grip around a rim.

do in the photo below. The roundness of the jaws generally won't damage the inner lip of a rim, but a wide rubber band such as a short length of tire inner tube that can expand with the jaws provides both protection for the wood and extra grip.

With some older or worn-out chucks, you might have a problem with the jaws expanding due to centrifugal force as you switch on the lathe. This would easily split many small bowls, so take care to stand to one side of the bowl as you hit the on switch.

Small bowls are easily mounted over expanding jaws. If the rim of the bowl is against the chuck, the bowl should run true.

Vacuum Chucks

A vacuum chuck holds the work by suction, pulling the bowl against or over a faceplate or form. They are wonderful for completing work that does not have obvious fixing points like the natural-edge bowl shown in the bottom photo at left.

A suitable vacuum pump can cost as much as two or three self-centering four-jaw chucks, so most people opt for the less expensive alternative of making their own using standard PVC pipe and an old vacuum cleaner. Many vacuum cleaners need some air flow to cool the motor, so it is common practice to puncture the hose two or three times with a fine point (like an escutcheon pin).

There are faceplates manufactured with a hose outlet attached (see the top photo on the facing page) or the air can be pulled through the hollow drive shaft in the headstock through a link outside the handwheel (see the bottom photo on the facing page). The manufactured faceplates typically have a thin, spongy rubber face for a better air seal. I prefer a harder surface that holds the bowl more firmly, so on the face-

This box elder bowl, 8 in. by 4⅞ in. (200mm by 125mm), was mounted over a vacuum chuck to complete the base.

For occasions when the rim of a bowl cannot fit flush with the faceplate or is likely to hit the headstock when fitting over the faceplate, I have a cardboard cylinder that fits into a groove on an MDF disc mounted on a standard faceplate.

plate shown in the top photo at right, I turned away most of the rubber to leave a layer about ³⁄₆₄ in. (1mm) thick. I also have several different-size MDF discs similar to those shown in the photo at right on the facing page with edges rounded to fit snugly against the inside of a bowl.

For occasions when the rim of the bowl cannot fit flush with the faceplate or is likely to hit the headstock when fitting over the faceplate, I mount the bowl over a cylinder, as in the bottom photo at right. I cut this short length of cardboard tube from a packing cylinder, then mounted it on a chuck on the lathe so I could turn the ends true. The cylinder fits into a groove turned in the MDF disc, and when the rim is sanded it becomes slightly fuzzy and provides a good seal. You can also use PVC drain pipe, but to soften the edge and provide a better seal, strap the rim with fabric surgical tape.

The bowls being chucked need to be solid, although small holes that would break the vacuum can temporarily be patched with masking tape or cling wrap. If you have a catch, a bowl is more likely to shift on the chuck than come off, but if you feel insecure, use tail-center support to ensure the job stays aligned while you do most of the work.

Finally

There are occasions when most turners will find each of these rechucking techniques useful. However, professionals tend to get set up for one approach and stick with that. Although that method will influence their designs, this is not necessarily disadvantageous. The important thing is to be able to make what you want to make. I am set up for footed bowls and have chucks that can grip almost any size foot. Any compromises I have to make are minimal.

If I want to remove a foot, it is no problem with the big bowl jaws, but so that I'm not changing jaws between each bowl I work in

The commercial vacuum faceplate (left) has a connecting hose for attaching a vacuum hose. My preferred connection is outboard, taking advantage of the hollow drive shaft (below). It consists of a turned nylon boss on the handwheel, over which the vacuum hose fits.

series, turning a batch of bowls one size before moving on to another size. Because most of my bowls can be easily remounted on one of my two sets of bowl jaws, I seldom use a vacuum faceplate. Other turners I know use the vacuum system all the time, whereas I keep it for natural-edge bowls.

Decide what you want to make, then find the route to that end that suits you best.

9 SANDING AND FINISHING

Finishing and what constitutes a so-called good finish occupy a good deal of space in woodworking magazines. Here I'll tell you how I go about things and why. I'm of the school that doesn't like glossy finishes: I proceed in the knowledge that wooden bowls subjected to ongoing use and careful maintenance soon look infinitely superior to those that sit on a shelf as decorative objects receiving the occasional dusting. To look its best, wood requires ongoing input.

Few of my customers are interested in unsanded bowls, no matter how good my toolwork or how interesting the textures I apply to my profiles. To achieve the silky smoothness most people seem to prefer on wood surfaces, you need to work through a range of abrasives, then apply a finish that brings out the color in the wood while making it even smoother. When my food bowls are going straight into use, I prefer not to apply any finish, but will wash them under hot running water with detergent, giving them the same treatment most cookware manufacturers demand for their products. I don't subject them to the dishwasher, although I know of bowls that survive dishwashers on a daily basis.

Sanding is not a stimulating activity, and I notice at woodturning symposiums that whenever a demonstrator reaches for abrasives half the audience rushes for the door, then reappears for the polishing and finishing techniques. Sanding might be boring to watch, but there's more to it than many people seem to realize. Finishing, on the other hand, can be comparatively simple.

Sanding might be boring, but there's more to it
than many people seem to realize.

Abrasives

Abrasives are graded by number according to the size of the cutting agent on the backing paper or cloth. The abrasives I use normally range from 60 grit (coarse) to 400 grit (fine) and these are either hand-held against the revolving wood or stuck to a pad for power-sanding using a drill or for rotary-sanding.

Abrasives and the way they can be used to sand bowls have come a long way in recent years. There was a time when you grabbed a bit of garnet paper, held it to the spinning wood, and worked slowly through the grades of abrasive using several sheets on a bowl. Sanding typically took twice as long as the turning. The best modern abrasives cut more aggressively and do not wear out as fast. They cost more, but they're well worth it.

I use silicon-carbide cloth-backed abrasives, which can be purchased by the roll or in shorter lengths off the roll. I find these cut better and longer than any paper-backed abrasives. Paper backing doesn't perform well in the extremes of humidity, becoming too floppy in the damp and too brittle in the dry. You need a light-weight backing material that remains flexible in all conditions and can be folded without creating a hard edge that can inflict deep scratches to the wood. For this reason, you should avoid any abrasive with a thick or stiff backing.

As you sand, proceed to a finer grade only when all marks from the previous grit are gone. You should see an even scoring pattern with no obvious deeper scratching before moving on. Keep the paper moving evenly and slowly across the work. If you jab or dab at the surface, you'll be sanding unevenly and increasing the likelihood of scratches.

I always use as much pressure as possible, constantly moving the abrasive. If you press too hard or too long in one place, the friction will heat the surface and induce cracks in almost any wood. Miniscule splits on end grain are typically a sign of sanding too long and hard in one

A sanding kit. The lump of crepe rubber on the lathe bed in front of the drills is an abrasives cleaner. Discs can be punched using a wad punch (rear). Scotch-brite sanding pads (right) are used in place of steel wool for fine-sanding beads. The rotary sanders (center front) leave the wood free of swirl marks and other sanding lines.

area. One way to limit the problem is to drop the lathe speed 10 percent to 15 percent, which is very easy if you have a variable-speed control but rather irritating if this involves groping for pulleys under the headstock. In the latter situation, most people carry on at the same speed and develop a more delicate touch. When tiny end-grain splits mar the surface, let the wood cool for a few minutes, then hand-sand with the grain, using fine abrasives (240 to 400 grit) and the lathe off.

Knowing which defects and torn grain you can realistically sand out comes with experience. Coarse abrasives—say, 36 grit—almost carve the wood away but not evenly. You shouldn't need to resort to such a brutal approach when gouges and chisels can do a much better job. Flowing curves are best achieved with tools, although small undulations can be removed with heavy sanding. The typical turned surface shown in the photo at

It's very easy to lose your original turned form as you sand,
making the definite indefinite and insipid.

The torn grain associated with some quilted figure (above) needs to be recut, whereas turning marks like those at right are easily sanded away.

right above sanded away easily, whereas the torn grain shown in the left photo above needed to be recut.

The first swipe of sanding will reveal all the high spots, broad bumps, spiral chatter marks, or concentric valleys. If you still have the wall thickness (courage and nerve might be needed as well), broad bumps are best turned away so you get a more flowing curve, although power-sanding with a large pad is an alternative.

It's very easy to lose your original turned form as you sand, making the definite indefinite and insipid. Beware of rounding edges that are better left crisp, as on a bowl or platter rim. Avoid rounding edges by sanding one surface first and then the other—never sand both together. But, for safety, remember to soften

the resultant sharp edge with a quick touch of fine abrasive. Crisp does not mean dangerously sharp.

Often when you finish sanding, the end grain will feel slightly rough as you run your hand back and forth across the wood surface. This occurs because the lathe rotates in one direction and the fibers have been bent in the opposite way. I usually hand-sand this problem away with the lathe at rest, but using a reversing switch on the lathe makes the job easier. If you can spin your lathe in the opposite direction, you can easily cut back all those bent fibers. The sanding sequence might then run: 80 grit forward/reverse, 100 grit reverse/forward, 180 grit forward/reverse, and polish normally. You can also raise the grain by wetting the surface with water or oil, then sanding the damp surface with wet-and-dry abrasives. This technique also limits dust.

When sanding with the lathe in reverse, there is always a chance of the chuck or faceplate unscrewing when you switch on the lathe unless there is a grub screw to prevent this from happening. When starting the lathe in reverse, I always spin the bowl by hand as I turn on the lathe.

Power-sanding speeds the process considerably, but it's not good around fine detail or in corners, so you need to know how to sand by hand.

Hand-Sanding

For hand-sanding I use 100 grit to 400 grit, resorting occasionally to old 60-grit sanding discs for torn grain, which often occurs in tight corners. These old discs continue to cut well long after they cease to be useful for power-sanding.

Use abrasives in pieces about 4½ in. by 6 in. (115mm by 150mm), and fold each one in three, as shown in the illustration at right, so that one cutting surface is not in contact with another. Additional benefits are that it's easier to hold and forms enough of a pad to protect your fingers from friction-generated heat, even when pressing fairly hard against the wood. Abrasive sheets folded over only once have a habit of unfolding and deteriorating more rapidly. Hold the folded sheet between your fingers and thumb and press it against the revolving wood, keeping the abrasive moving with even pressure.

When hand-sanding, it's easy to develop muscle strain, so it helps to get all the support you can from the lathe when sanding the outside of a bowl. In the photo at right, I lean on the headstock and use my left hand to pull my right hand, which holds the abrasive, against the wood. Whenever sanding around fine details, try to use the rest as a support.

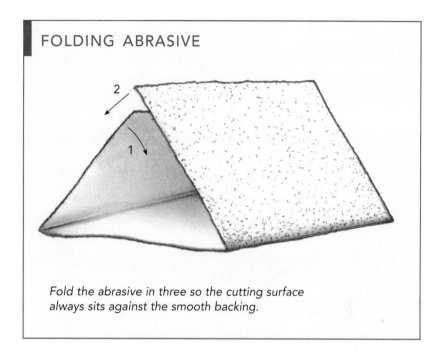

FOLDING ABRASIVE

Fold the abrasive in three so the cutting surface always sits against the smooth backing.

When hand-sanding, it is easy to develop muscle strain, so get all the support you can from the lathe; use your left hand to pull the right hand with the abrasive against the wood.

When sanding the inside of a bowl, use your left hand to equalize the pressure put against the wood by your right hand. If you use abrasives too aggressively without support, you can shatter a very fine bowl or pull it free of the chuck.

REMOVING LUMPS AND BUMPS

Abrasives can remove a great deal of material, so by sanding in one area, it's easy to create a dip. Remember also that the nearer center you get, the slower the wood is moving; comparatively little is removed near center, and a bump can easily develop. One advantage of power-sanding is that this is less likely to happen. To eliminate the bump when sanding by hand, stop the lathe and sand across center, rotating the lathe every other stroke. Then the center gets most of the attention.

Keep sanding pressure toward you when working on the inside and on top when working on the profile. Beware of letting your hand drift to the far side on the inside of shallow bowls. The upward rotation of the wood can grab the paper and carry your hand up to the top of the

bowl, from where it can shoot back to the far side to meet the upward swing of the wood. Your fingers are hit end-on, bent back, and can be broken. It all occurs in a fraction of a second, and is like diving onto concrete with fingertips extended. Or at least that's what it felt like.

Power-Sanding

For power-sanding, an abrasive disc is attached to a spongy foam backing pad mounted in an electric hand drill. Both abrasive and pad must be flexible to avoid scoring the wood, especially in tight concave curves. Most brands of abrasive discs are Velcro-backed, so these can be peeled on and off with ease. In addition to these, I use some adhesive-backed discs. The adhesive on these discs must be kept dust-free at all times, so when they're not in use on the drill I stick them on top of the lathe where the metal surface is easy to keep clear of dust.

Many people cut out their own discs using a wad punch (see the photo on p. 157), taking advantage of special deals on sheets of abrasives. You can punch through up to 10 sheets of the finer grit at once. (This is a good activity for days when nothing is going right and surplus aggression can be channeled into hitting the punch with a heavy hammer.)

The best tool for power-sanding is an angle drill, as shown in the top photos on the facing page, which can be used one-handed because the body of the drill lies at an angle to the surface being sanded. (Angle drills look like angle grinders but run much slower, at about 1,600 rpm.) A pneumatic angle sander is also excellent, but you need a big compressor to run it. Drills running about 1,800 rpm are much easier to handle than higher rpm tools.

A conventional pistol-grip drill seen in the bottom photo on the facing page is much less expensive but more difficult to handle and control because of a tendency to kick sideways. The trick to holding one firmly is to regard your left hand (nearer the sanding pad) as a fulcrum that

The best tool for power-sanding is an angle drill, which can also be used one-handed because the body of the drill lies at an angle to the surface being sanded.

stays more or less in one position, while the right hand pivots the sanding head around that point.

The position in which the disc is held against the wood varies the cutting power and the quality of the finished surface. The wood is normally revolving counterclockwise on the inboard side of the lathe. Most drills revolve clockwise, but you can use any portion of the disc for sanding. If you use the top or bottom, the grit will cut across the path of the rotating grain, leaving swirling score marks that are less obvious than the concentric score marks left when the disc travels against or with the wood. Typically you do the bulk of the sanding with each grit using the most aggressive cut, that is, with the disc rotating directly against the oncoming wood. As when hand-sanding, it pays to keep the tool moving across the surface to prevent heat buildup or excessive sanding in one spot, which will quickly flatten or dent that portion of your curve. When sanding the inside of a bowl, work in the bottom half, as shown in the top photo at right.

A conventional pistol-grip drill is difficult to control because of a tendency to kick sideways. The trick to holding them firmly is to regard your left hand (nearer the sanding pad) as a fulcrum that stays more or less in one position while the right hand pivots the sanding head around that point.

The major advantage of power-sanding, apart from speed, is that you can switch off the lathe and concentrate on a particularly difficult area of torn grain, smoothing it with much less effort than by hand. By sanding in a particular area, you'll create a slight dip, so once the torn area is removed, you'll need to restart the lathe and blend the indentation into the rest of the curve. Selecting a slower lathe speed helps.

If you sand a natural-edge bowl with the lathe running, the leading edge of each wing is sanded more aggressively, soon becoming thinner than the trailing edge. Natural-edge bowls look best when the bark rim is of even thickness. To sand any free-form rim, switch the lathe off and rotate the bowl (still on the lathe) back and forth by hand against the drill held firmly in a fixed position. This is relatively easy with an angle drill. The aim is to keep the tool steady as the wood sweeps past, so that the leading edges of an uneven rim are cut back no faster than those trailing. If a natural edge is somewhat uneven, use this technique to sand fatter parts of the rim to match the thinner so it all appears to be of even thickness, even though it might not be further down the bowl wall.

Alternatively, lock the drive shaft and sand with the bowl fixed in one position, as shown in the photo at left below.

Rotary-Sanding

Developed by Australian Kevin Davidson, the Rotary Sander looks like a cordless angle drill, but in fact it has no motor. The 3-in. (75mm) Rotary Sander has been copied and several versions have found their way into woodturning catalogs, but for me the original remains the best. The Rotary Sander works by freewheeling against the work as the lathe runs, removing clouds of dust and leaving few if any swirl marks because the abrasive moves mostly with the wood rather than across or against it (see the photo below).

Rotary-sanding is not as efficient as power-sanding for maintaining the curve across center, so I tend to use power-sanding for coarser grits and keep the Rotary Sander for 180 grit and finer.

Sand a natural edge with the lathe switched off to avoid uneven sanding of the rim.

Rotary-sanding is not as efficient as power-sanding, so I reserve this technique for 180 grit and finer. It leaves few if any swirl marks because the abrasive moves mostly with the wood rather than across or against it.

Oil-and-Wax Finishes

The top photo at right shows the ash and cherry bowls that have been in constant use in my home for 20 years. The one on the right is a favorite (see also the photo on p. 12) that I've used almost daily for a decade now for salads or hot potatoes or other vegetables. I sanded it originally but never applied a formal finish. Over the years, it has absorbed some salad dressing, but most of that has been removed as the bowl is washed in very hot water and detergent along with the pots and pans. (Wood can take this treatment.) The more it's used the smoother it gets, and as it ages it is becoming darker. It started out as a reddish pink like that shown in the photo on p. 122.

This is how I should like to see most of my bowls treated because I know that after only a few months of use they take on a different aura as their patina develops. Sealed or lacquered wood can never develop such a wonderful patina because nothing can penetrate the coated wood. But since few of my bowls go straight into domestic use, I have always preferred an oil-and-beeswax finish. The wax can easily be washed if the bowl is to be used for serving food; otherwise it provides a good base for further polishing with one of the many refurbishing polishes or oils available commercially.

Non-food bowls, which won't get wet but might store loose change, keys, jewelry, or any of that stuff we all have to keep somewhere, should be polished occasionally along with the filing bowls (those are bowls used for bits of paper) and others functioning as purely decorative objects. These soon take on a shinier persona, more like a polished antique as shown in the photo at right.

My preferred finish for all bowls is a mix of boiled linseed oil and pure beeswax. Apply the oil liberally with a soft cloth or brush with the lathe off. Next, start the lathe and press a lump of beeswax firmly against the revolving wood so that it melts on with the friction, leaving a thin

My preferred finish for all bowls is a mix of boiled linseed oil and pure beeswax.

The 13-in. (330mm)-diameter ash and 7½-in. (190mm) cherry bowls (left) have been in constant use for 20 years, the other for about a decade. The smooth, matte surface of the 9½-in. (240mm)-diameter Tasmanian myrtle bowl (right) is typical for any wood object constantly used and washed but never oiled or polished.

Always used as a fruit bowl, wiped occasionally, and polished even more occasionally, this bowl is aging well. Gray box, 1983, 12 in. (305mm) diameter.

The old rule of thumb for polishing wood is every day for a month, every week for a year, then every month thereafter.

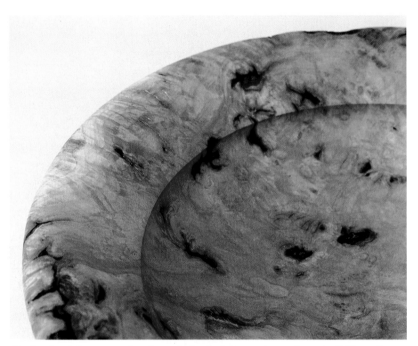

On burls with gum veins, I apply boiled linseed or mineral oil liberally, then a day later wipe away any surplus and hand-buff the surface with a soft cloth.

and visible layer on the surface. With the work still spinning, apply a rag firmly enough to melt the wax so that it either mixes with the oil in the wood or stays in the cloth. In time, the rag will become so impregnated with oil and wax that its application alone will be sufficient. I find the best rags come from old, soft, cotton shirts or underwear. If the work is delicate, absorb the pressure of the wax and rag in much the same way that you support thin work while turning or sanding. And remember never to wrap a finishing rag around your fingers in case it gets caught by the lathe.

I do not apply wax to any surfaces with splits or bark intrusions, such as the burl shown in the photo at left, because it builds up in drifts in the splits and is difficult to get rid of and looks terrible. Instead I set these bowls aside once the oil is applied so the oil can penetrate the wood and dry. After about 24 hours, I wipe off any oil remaining and hand-buff the surface. I apply another coat of oil and repeat the process as required, but a single oiling usually does the job.

In contrast to my oil-and-beeswax finish, hard waxes, such as carnauba, create problems. Hard wax is fine if the wood will always be polished—though it gives too high and hard a gloss for my taste—but it doesn't like water. Water or dampness can spot the surface, which will then have to be sanded off and re-oiled, a very difficult prospect for most people. It is a sad fact that many bowls are discarded once their glossy finish deteriorates—junk shops are full of them.

Most wood, regardless of how it's treated, will eventually become dark gold to reddish brown if polished or gray like a dead tree if left unfinished. Keep this in mind when you are busily bringing out the grain. It may be a great aid at the point of sale, but in the end you'll leave posterity with the shape to look at and the balance to feel—not the flashy finish.

Among my favorite handcrafted objects are the utilitarian 19th-century dairy and mixing bowls made by unknown craftsmen on primitive lathes in even more primitive conditions. Now mostly in museums, these pieces were made to a price for daily use, and typically the only finish would have been a quick burnish with a handful of shavings to buff up the shear-cut surface somewhat. Conventional finishing techniques were not responsible for the wonderful patina we admire, which is more the result of years of use, the soft abrasion of food-stuffs, and a skivvy's scrubbing brush—until some antique dealer applied a layer of primping polish in order to sell the bowl for more than the maker would have earned in a year. Clearly these bowls have wide appeal, most of which has to be the aura generated by the patina, since many of the forms are nothing special.

Unfortunately patina doesn't come in a bottle, but the oil-and-wax finish provides a good base for it. Wood can cope with a staggering amount in the way of knocks, cuts, and bruisings and look better for them, polishing up well despite any amount of abuse. Think of antique wooden planes and workbenches, the family breadboard, or furniture polished for a few decades. The first knock and stain might have been detrimental, but a thousand made the patina. The old rule of thumb for polishing wood is every day for a month, every week for a year, then every month thereafter. For this kind of finish, there are no short cuts (see the photos at right).

Sanding and finishing are two of the most subjective and controversial aspects of wood-turning. In general, it is better to learn to use your tools well; get a clean cut with chisel, gouge, or scraper; and keep the use of abrasives to a minimum. Whatever your inclination, I suggest you experiment to produce varied surfaces rather than the uniform, flat, plastic coating that smacks of technical more than aesthetic achievement. Perfection can be boring.

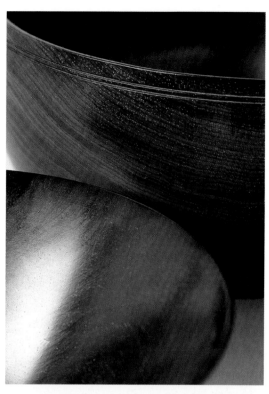

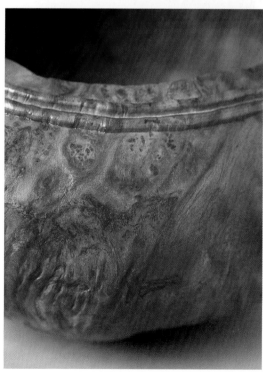

Regular polishing with furniture wax over a number of years has built on the original oil-and-beeswax finish.

10 DECORATION AND SURFACE

So far in this book I've discussed ways of turning basic forms. The creation of a good, strong, simple form turned from solid wood remains, for me, woodturning's greatest challenge. However, there are many times when a form needs that extra little something by way of a bead, groove, or texture to snap it into life. Or there may be some defect that you have to incorporate in your bowl when the alternative is losing the piece altogether. Or you might find some defects so striking that you want to include them into your overall design.

In this chapter, you'll see how to turn beads and grooves and how they can be used to enhance a profile while making a bowl easier to handle. Then there are sections on rims, some simple ways to add patterns and texture, and finally how I cope with defects.

Beads and Grooves

A bead is generally defined as a small, rounded molding sitting on a surface, like those shown in the left photo below, or in a corner as shown in

Beads can be practical as well as decorative in that they provide some purchase for your fingers when you lift a bowl. Set in a corner, as shown in the photo above, a bead adds strength when the bowl is very thin, while visually softening the angle.

If you round over the shoulders between grooves, you get inset beads.

You can cut grooves using either a spear-point scraper (top) or a small, shallow fingernail-ground gouge (above).

the photo at right on the facing page. As well as being decorative, beads can be practical in that they provide some purchase for your fingers as you lift a bowl, especially when a bowl is large and you need to use both hands.

Grooves are V-shaped incisions that appear as lines in a surface. They are much easier to turn than beads, although often they have just as much visual impact. Grooves were tradition-ally used by bowl turners to decorate a profile and, like beads, often made heavier bowls easier to grip when lifting them. If you round over the wood between two grooves, you get inset beads like those shown in the photo above.

Grooves can be turned using a spear-point scraper as shown in the top photo at left, although the wood will be cut more cleanly using a ⅜-in. (9mm) shallow gouge with a long fingernail edge, as shown in the bottom photo at left. The cut is very similar to cutting a foot. Align the bevel in the direction you want to cut with the flute facing away from the wood. Start with the handle low, then raise the handle to pivot the edge into the wood. The tool should pivot on the rest, not move forward across it.

Cutting Beads on a Profile

For beads that sit proud of the bowl profile, start with a raised section that's sized for the number of beads you intend to form. Then cut the beads using a ⅜-in. shallow gouge with a long finger-nail-ground edge. This is the best tool for the job.

1 Start the gouge almost on its side to avoid a catch.

2 Then drop the handle and roll the tool slightly clockwise to cut the right side of the bead.

3 At the same time, use your right hand (on the handle) to start circling the handle counterclockwise, which brings the edge to the top of the bead. To cut a nice round bead, the trick is to keep the edge at the same angle as you cut up one side and down the other, pivoting the edge into the wood.

4 As you near the end of the cut, roll the gouge onto its side again as the handle is brought near horizontal.

Then repeat the action from the opposite direction to complete the groove.

Beads are most easily turned in a similar way using a ⅜-in. (9mm) shallow gouge with a long fingernail edge. If beads are to sit on a surface, turn the curve on which they'll sit, leaving a raised mass for the beads, then turn the beads, as shown in the photos on the facing page. If you roll the gouge at the top of the bead to cut into the wood, which seems logical and is often done, you'll actually create an angle rather than a smooth, convex curve.

To cut the next bead, move the tool a bead-width along the rest, pivoting the tool on its nose, which must maintain its position at the bottom of the bead just cut. Then repeat the process by dropping the handle as you roll the tool clockwise and so on. As you cut a series of beads, the end of the tool handle should make small circles counterclockwise, one for each bead.

If you need to clean up around the base of a bead, use a spear-point scraper. Beads on a surface look better if the corners at their base are detailed with a very small groove. Use the spear-point scraper very gently, keeping it flat on the rest. A tiny groove will also make sanding into the base of the bead and maintaining a flowing profile curve easier.

To cut a groove on a face, where you cut across the end grain rather than into it, you need a slightly different technique than on a profile. All cuts should be made from the face into the wood, as shown in the top photo at right, where I cut in from either side to turn a groove that decorates the bottom of a bowl.

To make an inset bead on a face, first cut a groove, as described above. Then, with the gouge on its side, ride the bevel shoulder on the wood to the left of the groove and position the edge on what will be the top of the bead (see the center photo at right. The gouge remains on

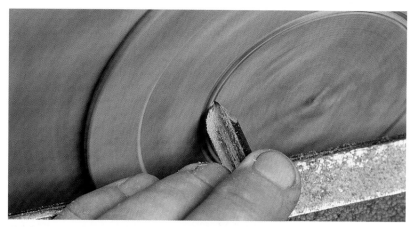

Cutting a groove to decorate the bottom of a bowl, I always use a ⅜-in. (9mm) fingernail-ground shallow gouge.

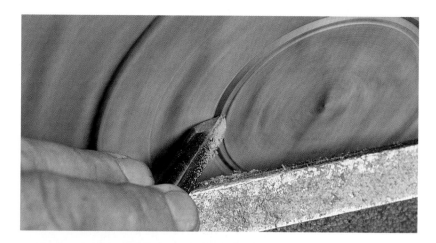

To turn an inset bead, begin with a groove and ride the bevel shoulder of the gouge on the wood to the left of the groove. Keep the gouge facing sideways, as you pivot the edge into the wood to cut the right side of the bead. Then cut from the right to clean the right side of the second groove.

To create a bead on a rim, turn the surface either side of the bead, then use small arcing cuts to round the bead.

CUTTING A COVE ON A FACE

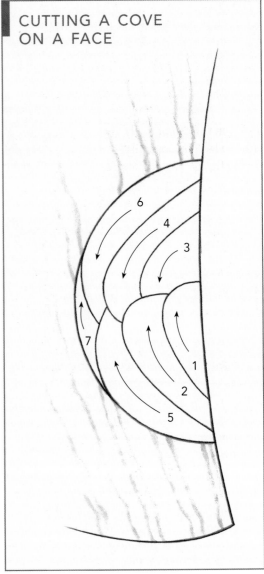

CUTTING A BEAD ON A FACE

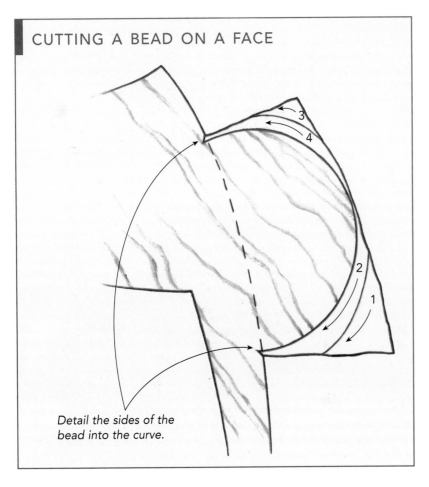

Detail the sides of the bead into the curve.

its side as you pivot it into the wood to cut the right-hand side of the bead (see the bottom photo on p. 169). Any angle or facet on top of the bead can be rounded with small arcing cuts or abrasives.

If you want to create a bead that sits on a bowl rim, as shown in the photo at left above, turn the surface on either side of the bead, then make small arcing cuts from the top of the bead (see the illustration at left).

To turn a cove into a flat rim or base, use a fingernail-ground shallow gouge, cutting in from either side, as shown in the illustration at right on the facing page. The gouge is presented as for an inset bead. Then, as the cuts proceed toward the bottom, roll the gouge slightly so that at the bottom of the cove the flute faces up.

One of the simplest forms of decoration for a base is an inset dome or large flattish bead like one of those shown in the photo below. These are very simple to turn by easing the sharp corner of a scraper into the wood.

Rims

The rim is an important part of a bowl that affects the way the bowl feels as well as looks. On heavier bowls, a fat, rounded rim can feel so good you might not want to put the bowl down. On finer forms, some sort of a bead might be a better solution.

A rim can be textured and burned so it becomes a frame that contrasts with the working (containing) part of the bowl (see the photo below). If the bowl is very large or heavy such as shown in the bottom photo, an overhanging rim makes it much easier to grasp, while reduc-

The simplest form of decoration for a base is an inset dome, turned by easing the sharp corner of a scraper into the wood. Here the end of the rounded left side of a shear scraper has been ground to create the sharp corner.

Burned and textured rims contrast with and frame the working (containing) part of the bowl.

If a bowl is very large or heavy, an overhanging rim makes it much easier to pick up. It also reduces the weight of the piece without reducing the overall size. Jarrah burl, 21 in. by 5 in. (535mm by 130mm).

Rims can be varied infinitely.
Here are a few starting points.

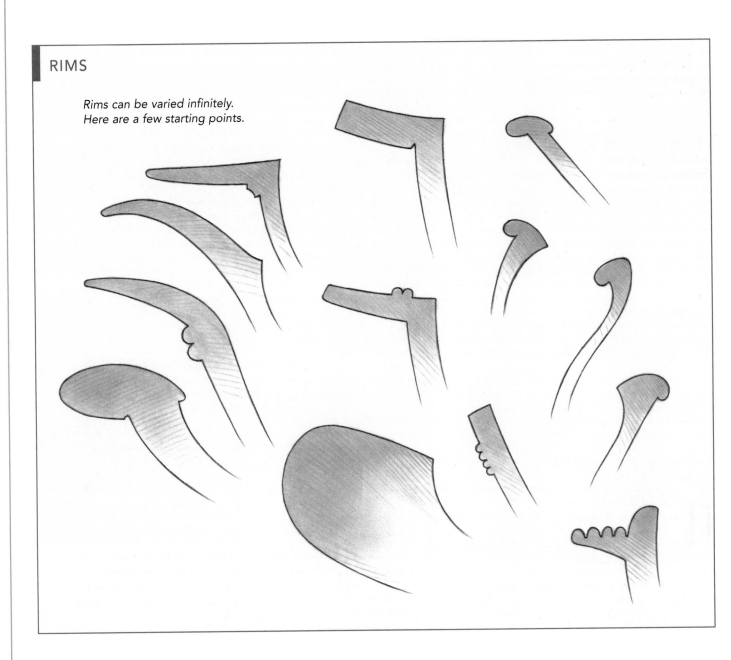

ing the weight of the piece without reducing the overall size.

When the rim overhangs the bowl wall, I like to detail the angle between the two. I sometimes use a bead, as shown in the photo at right on p. 166, but if this doesn't appeal, try what is in effect a small V-groove by continuing the curve of one surface into the other, as shown in the top photo at left on the facing page. In each case, I create a definite line where the rim contacts the wall, making the design a more positive statement.

As the jarrah bowl shown in the top photo at right on the facing page seasoned, it warped much more than expected. Not wishing to lose the overall dimensions, I retained the warped form, treating it as a natural-edge bowl. When finished, the bowl looked particularly bland, with the rim difficult to determine. The blackened rim provides a more defined edge while

By continuing the curve of one surface into that of the other, you create a small V-cut; the definite line where the rim contacts the wall makes for a positive design statement.

Charring defined the rim and made all the difference on this otherwise stark form. Jarrah, 18 in. (460mm) diameter.

A beaded rim is a nice detail. The soft chamfer on the inner edge feels comfortable when you hook your thumb over the rim to pick up the bowl.

An undercut inner lip is a good way to define the inner space of a bowl. Cut this using a skewed scraper very gently, and be sure to keep the tool flat on the rest to avoid a catch. To limit vibration as the bowl wall thins, lower the speed about 200 rpm.

emphasizing its eccentricity. Any eccentric rim looks best when of even thickness.

In the photo above, a beaded rim is a nice detail. The soft chamfer on the inner edge of each bowl feels comfortable when you hook your thumb over the rim to pick up the bowl.

An undercut inner lip (see the photo at right above) is a good way of defining the inner space. Cut these using a skewed scraper very gently, and be sure to keep the tool flat on the rest to avoid a catch. To limit vibration as the bowl wall thins, reduce the speed about 200 rpm.

Texture

The ultrasmooth and glossy surfaces achieved through fine sanding and hard finishes are all very well, but such perfection can be boring. I always enjoy a finish straight from the gouge.

An easy way to create a textured surface is to
hold a wire brush against the wood as it spins on the lathe.

This bowl was turned green and the wood cut so cleanly that it seemed a pity to destroy the surface with abrasives. As the bowl dried, it distorted somewhat, crinkling the beads and surface. Jarrah, 7 in. by 4 in. (180mm by 100mm).

This is an assortment of abrasive-impregnated nylon-bristle brushes used for texturing and cleaning out bark intrusions and holes.

I turned the beaded jarrah bowl shown in the photo above green, and the wood cut so cleanly that it seemed a pity to destroy the surface with abrasives, so I left it to dry unsanded. As the bowl dried, it distorted somewhat, crinkling the beads and surface. I rounded the bottom of the bowl to accommodate some warping, but in fact it sits firmly on a flat surface. It was tempting to take the beads lower down the profile, but I think the beadless base looks better. Note the smooth band below the rim. If you take the beads all the way to the top, rarely does it look right. Moreover, you have no margin for error as you turn the top of the rim and make the final internal cuts.

An easier way to create a textured surface is to hold a wire brush against the wood as it spins on the lathe. This removes all the softer grain, creating a canvaslike surface on a tight-grained wood. Better still is a drill-mounted wire brush (see the photo above). You can use these brushes to create more subtle textures, sanding across the rotating wood, as well as directly against it. Before applying a wire brush, sand the surface to 100 grit; otherwise any torn grain will be highlighted. When using a drill-mounted brush, lower the lathe speed so the brush can cut more effectively. For a smoother finish, I complete the brushing using Nyalox abrasive-impregnated nylon bristle.

When applying bands of texture, as shown in the top photo at right, do the texturing first, then the sanding, taking care not to let the abrasives touch the textured surfaces.

On open-grained woods such as ash or elm, sandblasting etches out the softer grain more drastically than any brush (see the bottom photo at right. In preparation for sandblasting, the surface needs to be devoid of scratches because the process doesn't eliminate these. For those interested in much coarser and more robust surfaces, there are texturing tools commercially available, such as the Sorby Spiraling System, which can be used to create a variety of swirling patterns and spirals.

More laboriously, you can carve patterns into a surface using a mallet and chisel, a power-carving tool, or a high-speed grinder such as a Dremel tool seen in the top right photo on p. 176. The same Dremel tool was used to make the dots on the bead in the top left photo on p. 176. I feel that working freehand imparts more energy to the finished bowl, but for more precise work I can mount the Dremel or an angle grinder in a cross-slide set on a table that mounts into the tool-rest banjo.

The dots and other small marks are cut on or between pencil lines drawn on the bowl before it's sanded. Sanding then removes the layout lines and defines the rim of the marks precisely, eliminating any evidence of the cutter not entering the wood smoothly. A ring of dots on their own can look a bit lost, so I'll typically enclose these within a pair of grooves.

Very heavy sanding on open-grained timber can develop an undulating surface that echoes the wear of decades of use. But I find I can remove more material by burning the surface using a gas torch before sanding. The technique works particularly well with burls and rough

The textured band in the bowl was made holding a wire brush against the bottom of a flat recess, the sides of which were cut but not sanded.

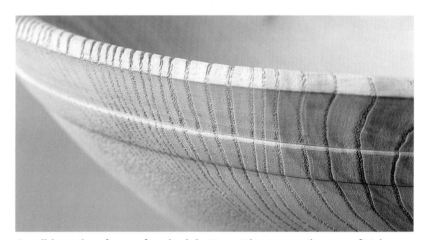

Sandblasted surfaces often look better without any oil or wax finish. The wood is ash.

split lumps from which there is no hope of making a defect-free bowl. By leaving some of the charred surface and cutting through to the bright wood elsewhere, it is possible to create a striking bowl like that shown in the bottom photo at right on p. 176. Such material needs to be left thick or it flies apart, and sanding away the charred surface to reveal patches of the natural wood is a messy business, even with good dust extraction.

Using different bits mounted in a high-speed grinder, you can carve a range of dots and lines with ease.

After several hours and three variations, there was not enough thickness remaining in the rim for heavy carving, so I settled for a slightly charred surface, which I think looks better anyway. Jarrah, 19½ in. (495mm) diameter.

After I sanded the surface to 100 grit, I charred the surface of this heavy-walled bowl using a propane gas torch, then sanded again, cutting through the charred surface in some areas to allow the color of the wood to emerge. Red gum, 12 in. (305mm) diameter.

However, the journey toward the end product is usually exciting because you never know precisely how it will work out. The trick becomes knowing when to stop, but if the bowl doesn't look too good, all you do is sand back to char-free wood and start again. More often than not, lumps of wood full of patches of rot and other intrusive defects can meld into a charac-

terful whole if you work the surface enough. The large bowl shown in the photo at left above looked gross after I'd gashed the rim and didn't improve much with heavy burning and sanding. I tried several carved versions of the rim, turning away each until I ran out of wood. I prefer the plainer end result.

The enjoyable part of working on this sort of piece is that you can put it back on the lathe and remove the bits you don't like and try something else. You are limited only by your imagination, and you can incorporate all manner of materials, although whether the result should be submitted to public gaze is another matter. I have a number of bowls in progress that as I write don't look as though they'll ever go beyond the workshop, but making them has been an enriching experience.

Color

You can alter the appearance of a bowl with color, and a number of books have been written on coloring bowls and woodturnings in general. In 1981 I had an exhibition in London of holly bowls stained bright colors. Wittily entitled "Holly Wood in London," it was my response to pressure to make something different—to show that my work was advancing and breaking new ground and not atrophying. The bowls sold well enough, but I was left wondering if the addition of color really did much to enhance the forms. Was I trying to imitate ceramics? Was I being true to the wood, let alone myself?

The next time I used color was in 1996 at a woodturners' gathering in Canada, when I sprayed the small elm bowl shown in the top photo at right. Although I thoroughly enjoyed the experience, I still felt that if I'm going to use paint I'd rather work on a canvas to hang on a wall. But then I did leave school intending to be an artist.

So while using color on bowls isn't for me, some turners use it to great effect. One of the best is Michael Hosaluk, who in a collaborative session took my small, four-sided jarrah bowl and transformed it by cutting into one corner and decorating the rim with a pyrographic tool and paint (see the bottom photo at right).

By coloring bowls, you can emulate ceramics. Elm with color lacquer, 7½ in. (185mm) diameter.

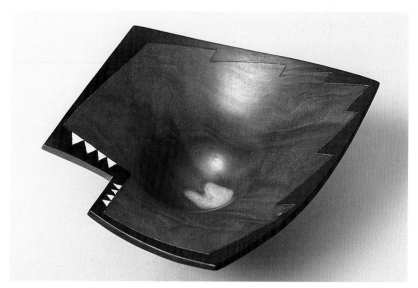

During a collaborative session, Canadian Michael Hosaluk took my small, straight-sided bowl and transformed it by cutting into one corner and decorating the edge. It's been used as a ring bowl ever since.

Holes, Bark Inclusions, and Recut Forms

I began turning wood when a defect was a defect and not the basis for a work of art, as it often is today. When making thin, classic forms, I still feel uncomfortable including splits and bark intrusions in a bowl that is otherwise of solid timber. However, the increasing scarcity

Grevillea Silky Oak Bowls

Small, dull, round bowls with splits are prime material for experiment; reshaped on the bandsaw and sanded, these manage to stay out of the log basket. Others have been destroyed as I tried to add interest to dull forms and wood, but the process was always stimulating.

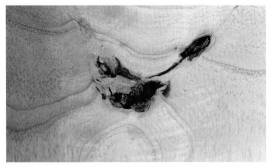

The black portions of this bark intrusion are fine dark sawdust fixed in place with cyanoacrylate adhesive.

MATERIAL:	Grevillea silky oak
SIZES:	5½ in. (140mm) diameter, 6⅝ in. (170mm) diameter

One advantage of coming to terms with a defect is that you get to explore some dramatically different forms.

of good-quality material and the market acceptance of (and even desire for) pieces that include features previously regarded as undesirable has meant that I now use timber I would formerly have avoided, and I've learned to deal with the defects.

For many years, modern adhesives and epoxy have made it possible to fill and stabilize smaller splits and knots so that they look as though they've always been solid. I pack narrow splits and openings that run with the grain with very fine dust from dark wood, then bond it together with a few drops of thin cyanoacrylate adhesive (commonly called Super Glue). To ensure an even bonding as the resin percolates the dust, I spray accelerator into the split before filling the hole. I find that African blackwood does the best job, looking just like the remnants of a forest fire or natural staining, but cocobolo and many of the very dark Australian acacias or black powder paint are almost as good.

When the space to be filled is more than ⅛ in. (3mm) wide, I'll stuff in lengths of shavings or wood chips before packing in the fine dust so that it's possible to simulate a bark intrusion. Fill the defects after you've trued the form so you don't waste too much of the very expensive adhesive.

One advantage of coming to terms with a defect is that you get to explore some dramatically different forms like that shown in the photo below. Here I gave up trying to eliminate the bark intrusion, feeling that the holes wouldn't look too bad on the inner lip of the rim. It is possible to view the bowl and be unaware of the holes, which then give the piece a whole new dimension when the bowl is viewed from above.

With some burls, chunks are likely to fall off as work proceeds, as was the case with the red gum bowl shown in the photo at right below. Rather than reduce the height of the bowl, I decided to sand the rim aggressively, rounding

the shoulders at either end of the broken section. By power-sanding with the lathe running at around 200 rpm, the sander can follow the undulating rim, softening all the edges.

Single splits, like the heart shakes typical from the center of a log, can be used to advantage provided they are symmetrical and aligned across the center of the blank. The blank for the bird's-eye maple bowl shown in the bottom left photo split along the pith, which fortunately was in the center of the blank. I turned this bowl ignoring the split, knowing I would detail it later.

In coming to terms with a bark intrusion, I developed what was for me an entirely new form. I failed to eliminate the defect, but I have a bowl that can be viewed without the holes or from above, which gives the piece a whole new aspect. Gidgee, 6¼ in. by 3 in. (160mm by 75mm).

Rather than reduce the height of this bowl, I decided to sand the rim aggressively, rounding the shoulders at either end of the broken section. Red gum, 10 in. (255mm) diameter.

Each of these bowls had a split along the grain. Because the split was on the diameter, symmetrical detailing of the rim was possible. Left: Birdseye maple, 12 in. by 4 in. (305mm by 100mm). Above: Sally wattle, 8 in. by 2½ in. (200mm by 65mm).

AFTERWORD: Design, Form, Balance, and the Marketplace

Woodturning is a very seductive activity, and when you begin to turn bowls, you have to be careful not to get carried away by the ease with which you can create all manner of curves, ogees, beads, and coves. I did so myself until I realized that I was becoming preoccupied with what I could do on the lathe, rather than creating worthwhile objects that would earn me a living and build me a reputation.

One of the ongoing challenges for me is creating well-balanced bowls that not only look good but also feel good when you pick them up. It is very easy to get the physical weight concentrated uncomfortably in the base or rim. Or you might create a fine, even wall thickness, only to have the bowl look as though it's one of a million molded in plywood in some vast, anonymous factory. I don't think there is any particular virtue in having an even wall thickness, but it's good to make a few so you know you can do it.

Creating a fancy profile with all manner of angles and beads is enjoyable, and in workshops I see students glowing with satisfaction, at least halfway through such a project. For the problem then arises as to what shape the inside should be so it relates to the outside, and how can you distribute the weight so the bowl feels good when you pick it up. Shown in the photo below are the remains of two better-than-usual novice bowls. Each was well finished, and the upper one felt good in the hand, whereas the lower one did not, although the curves flow as curves should. The maker of the lower bowl went for even wall thickness, then realized the need to lighten the base. A lower foot would have solved his balance problem. The maker of the upper bowl had the wood breaking away around the foot because he had the chuck expending within the recess, whereas it should have closed around the central boss. These are what I term "just miss" bowls.

Commonly, turned bowls would be dramatically better had their curves curved without the sort of flat sections, dips, or bumps evident in the top left photo on the facing page. On the upper bowl, the inner curve changes direction rather than bending about one-third of the way down, while

The creation of a simple bowl that looks good and also feels good in the hand remains an ongoing challenge. A good, simple bowl is not so simple to make. Gidgee, 6½ in. (165mm) diameter.

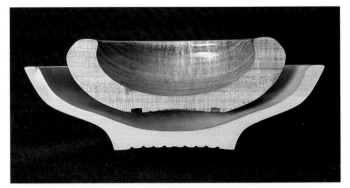

Both these novice bowls were well finished, but the one on top broke at the rim of the base, stressed by expanding chuck jaws. The lower bowl looked top-heavy and didn't feel very nice when handled.

the profile dips in the lower half. Physically, the balance is okay. The lower bowl also has the hint of a dip in the bottom half of the profile, while the inside curve is almost straight at the top before it takes a shortcut to the base. The center dip is typically the result of oversanding.

When the curves flow as curves should, the crucial differences between bowls lie in the precise wall thickness and the relationship between the inner and profile curves. In the photo at right below, the lower bowl with its uneven wall felt much better balanced in the hand; the upper bowl felt fat and cumbersome by comparison, although there seems very little difference between the two.

On wide-rimmed bowls, such as that shown in the bottom photo at left below, it pays to keep the rim very slightly thicker than the lower wall because the bowl will be lifted by the rim, frequently using only one hand. A thin rim might not take the strain. The small bead on the profile between the rim and the lower profile adds a bit of mass and strength where it's needed.

The slightly tapering wall of the upper bowl shown in the bottom photo at right below feels the better of the two. In these outflowing forms, one anticipates that the weight will be toward the base.

The inside of a sharply angled profile, such as that shown on the left in the top left photo on p. 182, needs to echo the

Very commonly, turned bowls would have been dramatically better had their curves curved, without flats, dips, bumps, and other odd changes in direction.

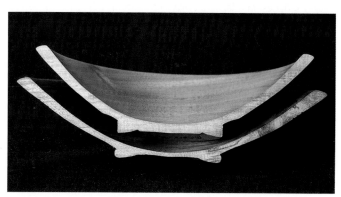

The lower bowl, with its uneven wall, felt much better balanced in the hand; the upper bowl's wall felt fat and cumbersome by comparison, although there seems very little difference between the two.

On a large wide-rimmed bowl—this one is 15 in. (380mm) across—it pays to keep the rim very slightly thicker than the lower wall because the bowl will be lifted by the rim, frequently by only one hand.

The slightly tapering wall of the upper bowl feels the better of the two. In these outflowing forms we expect the weight to be toward the base.

My approach to design is to keep the basic forms simple, adding occasional beads or grooves to the profile and rim to adjust proportions.

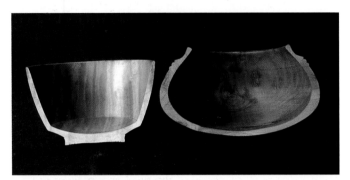

The inside of a sharply angled profile like that on the left needs to echo the outside. The enclosed form, right, felt well balanced. Even better would be to have the upper wall slightly thinner and the base marginally thicker for greater stability.

The only real difference between these bowls is that the upper curve of the one on the right comes in slightly more than that of the other, but that small difference makes the bowl on the right a much better piece.

A curve should flow unaffected by a groove or other feature cut into it. Sally wattle, 13 in. (330mm) diameter.

outside. The enclosed form shown on the right felt well balanced, although even better would be to have the upper wall slightly thinner and the base marginally thicker for greater stability.

My approach to design is to keep the basic forms simple, adding occasional beads or grooves to the profile and rim to adjust proportions, after which I consider adding texture or

charring the surface. You can usually apply beads or grooves with equal visual effect. The difference is that beads, especially when set on the form, are more difficult to turn. Still, if you make a mess of your beads, you can always turn them into a groove or two instead.

If the profile is simple, it should be easy to create a complementary inside. However, simple shapes are not half as simple as they look, especially given that, to look really good, a curve should flow unaffected by any beads sitting on it or grooves cut into it.

Asymmetric curves are generally more interesting than portions of a circle, but how these are set in relation to the base or foot determines whether the bowl will look heavy or light. An interesting exercise is to make similar bowls with slight variations, like those shown in the photo above.

In a similar vein, the convex curve from the base of the bowl shown in the top right photo on the facing page makes for a full and practical form, whereas the slight ogee into the foot shown in the top left photo on the facing page raises the form, making it look more ornamental. So while the upper sections of each profile as well as the diameters of the two bases are nearly identical, the narrower approach to the foot makes a world of difference in the character of the bowls.

The upper section of each of these profiles is nearly identical, and so is the diameter of each base. But the ogee foot makes the bowl at left more decorative compared with the fuller, more practical shape of the bowl above. River red gum, approximately 10 in. (255mm) diameter.

The more open shape of the bowl on the right leaves the form looking rather top heavy compared with the bowl on the left, which is also far more pleasing around the rim, making it the better of the two. Gidgee, approximately 6 in. (150mm) diameter.

These bowls are very similar inside and functionally will do the same job, but they feel quite different. The convex facets of the upper bowl give the whole bowl a softer appearance, while the concave upper facet in the lower bowl makes for a more defined angle and a harder line. Tasmanian blackwood, 10 in. to 11 in. (255mm to 280mm) diameter.

Another subtle but consequential difference: The more open shape of the bowl shown on the right in the photo above leaves the form looking rather top-heavy. By comparison, the bowl on the left is far more pleasing around the rim, making it the better of the two.

The bowls with angled profiles shown in the center and bottom photos at right are very similar inside and functionally will do the same job. When the facets are convex as seen in the center photo, it is very difficult to create a precise angle between the facets, and consequently the whole bowl has a softer feel about it as light settles on the curves. In contrast,

Always cost your wood at the
higher end of current replacement value.

note how the concave upper facet seen in the bottom photo on p. 183 makes for a more defined angle and harder line.

When judging a bowl, it's a good idea to do so directly in relation to other similar bowls. It is difficult to assess or criticize anything in isolation because it is only good or bad in relation to something comparable. If you belong to a woodturning group, a good project is to have everyone make a simple bowl following a drawing, then line them all up and discuss why some look better than others. The reasons will lie in the sort of differences seen between the two sets of bowls discussed above. Woodturners don't do enough of this sort of thing.

Selling Your Bowls

The marketplace is the best place there is to find out what people really think of your work. Be warned that this can be very sobering to hurtful. But the feedback is always useful, particularly if you want to earn a living as a turner.

In selling your bowls, unless you desperately need the money, don't underprice them. This is a plea on behalf of professional turners everywhere who suffer from hobby turners aiming only to "cover costs." Work offered for sale at a price less than the value of the raw materials is common and a great disservice to craftspeople struggling to make a living. It leads consumers to expect similar bargains all the time.

The basic price for a bowl is worked out by charging an amount for the time taken to make it, plus the *current* value of the raw materials (wood, abrasives, finish), plus an amount for fixed costs (equipment, power, insurance, taxes). This is a wholesale cost: the cost at which work sells to a retailer who will add from 80 percent to 150 percent to your price. To this, most turners will add a bit more for dramatic grain or what they might feel is a superior piece of artwork. How much more you load a wholesale price is between you and your ego and what the market can stand. You'll be surprised at what the market can and cannot stand.

My rule of thumb for calculating how long it should take to turn a bowl works surprisingly well for those above 6 in. (150mm) in diameter turned from seasoned wood. Working in inches, multiply the diameter by the height to get the approximate time the bowl should take in minutes. For example: 10 in. x 3 in. = 30 minutes. Working in centimeters is the same, except that you divide the result by six: 25.5cm x 7.5cm = 187.6 divided by 6 = 31.25 minutes. For enclosed forms, I allow one-third more time. All my wholesale prices are based on these calculations rather than on how long I actually take.

Always cost your wood at the higher end of current replacement value, not the price you paid for it. If you acquired it for less, or for nothing, that's a bonus for you.

You can also price your bowls by matching prices for similar bowls displayed in galleries and retail stores. But remember, if you see a bowl sitting on a shelf month after month, it's either too expensive or in the wrong outlet.

In the commercial world, you will invoice the retailer for the goods and (in theory) be paid within 30 days. In practice, payment can often be delayed and occasionally difficult to collect. Nevertheless, expect retailers to require you to deliver on time. I have a policy of exchanging bowls that fail to sell, taking them back if in good condition. What fails to sell in one situation will always sell somewhere else, but goods sitting on a gallery shelf month after month is bad for everybody.

Many galleries insist on a sale-or-return arrangement, which might be fair enough if your work is very expensive, eccentric, or unusual and possibly difficult to sell. But I have always resisted such an arrangement, feeling that retailers should borrow working capital from bankers rather than from me in the form of free stock.

In the final analysis, if your customer thinks he or she is getting a bargain, or at least very good value for the money, while you think you're getting a fair (or more than fair) return for your efforts, you have got things right.

INDEX

Index note: page references in *italics* indicate a photograph; page references in **bold** indicate an illustration.